FREE Test Taking Tips DVD Offer

To help us better serve you, we have developed a Test Taking Tips DVD that we would like to give you for FREE. **This DVD covers world-class test taking tips that you can use to be even more successful when you are taking your test.**

All that we ask is that you email us your feedback about your study guide. Please let us know what you thought about it – whether that is good, bad or indifferent.

To get your **FREE Test Taking Tips DVD**, email freedvd@studyguideteam.com with "FREE DVD" in the subject line and the following information in the body of the email:

   a. The title of your study guide.

   b. Your product rating on a scale of 1-5, with 5 being the highest rating.

   c. Your feedback about the study guide. What did you think of it?

   d. Your full name and shipping address to send your free DVD.

If you have any questions or concerns, please don't hesitate to contact us at freedvd@studyguideteam.com.

Thanks again!

Praxis Reading Specialist Study Guide 5301

Praxis II Reading Specialist 5301 Test Prep & Practice Test Questions

Test Prep Books Reading Specialist Exam Team

Table of Contents

Quick Overview

As you draw closer to taking your exam, effective preparation becomes more and more important. Thankfully, you have this study guide to help you get ready. Use this guide to help keep your studying on track and refer to it often.

This study guide contains several key sections that will help you be successful on your exam. The guide contains tips for what you should do the night before and the day of the test. Also included are test-taking tips. Knowing the right information is not always enough. Many well-prepared test takers struggle with exams. These tips will help equip you to accurately read, assess, and answer test questions.

A large part of the guide is devoted to showing you what content to expect on the exam and to helping you better understand that content. In this guide are practice test questions so that you can see how well you have grasped the content. Then, answer explanations are provided so that you can understand why you missed certain questions.

Don't try to cram the night before you take your exam. This is not a wise strategy for a few reasons. First, your retention of the information will be low. Your time would be better used by reviewing information you already know rather than trying to learn a lot of new information. Second, you will likely become stressed as you try to gain a large amount of knowledge in a short amount of time. Third, you will be depriving yourself of sleep. So be sure to go to bed at a reasonable time the night before. Being well-rested helps you focus and remain calm.

Be sure to eat a substantial breakfast the morning of the exam. If you are taking the exam in the afternoon, be sure to have a good lunch as well. Being hungry is distracting and can make it difficult to focus. You have hopefully spent lots of time preparing for the exam. Don't let an empty stomach get in the way of success!

When travelling to the testing center, leave earlier than needed. That way, you have a buffer in case you experience any delays. This will help you remain calm and will keep you from missing your appointment time at the testing center.

Be sure to pace yourself during the exam. Don't try to rush through the exam. There is no need to risk performing poorly on the exam just so you can leave the testing center early. Allow yourself to use all of the allotted time if needed.

Remain positive while taking the exam even if you feel like you are performing poorly. Thinking about the content you should have mastered will not help you perform better on the exam.

Once the exam is complete, take some time to relax. Even if you feel that you need to take the exam again, you will be well served by some down time before you begin studying again. It's often easier to convince yourself to study if you know that it will come with a reward!

Test-Taking Strategies

1. Predicting the Answer

When you feel confident in your preparation for a multiple-choice test, try predicting the answer before reading the answer choices. This is especially useful on questions that test objective factual knowledge. By predicting the answer before reading the available choices, you eliminate the possibility that you will be distracted or led astray by an incorrect answer choice. You will feel more confident in your selection if you read the question, predict the answer, and then find your prediction among the answer choices. After using this strategy, be sure to still read all of the answer choices carefully and completely. If you feel unprepared, you should not attempt to predict the answers. This would be a waste of time and an opportunity for your mind to wander in the wrong direction.

2. Reading the Whole Question

Too often, test takers scan a multiple-choice question, recognize a few familiar words, and immediately jump to the answer choices. Test authors are aware of this common impatience, and they will sometimes prey upon it. For instance, a test author might subtly turn the question into a negative, or he or she might redirect the focus of the question right at the end. The only way to avoid falling into these traps is to read the entirety of the question carefully before reading the answer choices.

3. Looking for Wrong Answers

Long and complicated multiple-choice questions can be intimidating. One way to simplify a difficult multiple-choice question is to eliminate all of the answer choices that are clearly wrong. In most sets of answers, there will be at least one selection that can be dismissed right away. If the test is administered on paper, the test taker could draw a line through it to indicate that it may be ignored; otherwise, the test taker will have to perform this operation mentally or on scratch paper. In either case, once the obviously incorrect answers have been eliminated, the remaining choices may be considered. Sometimes identifying the clearly wrong answers will give the test taker some information about the correct answer. For instance, if one of the remaining answer choices is a direct opposite of one of the eliminated answer choices, it may well be the correct answer. The opposite of obviously wrong is obviously right! Of course, this is not always the case. Some answers are obviously incorrect simply because they are irrelevant to the question being asked. Still, identifying and eliminating some incorrect answer choices is a good way to simplify a multiple-choice question.

4. Don't Overanalyze

Anxious test takers often overanalyze questions. When you are nervous, your brain will often run wild, causing you to make associations and discover clues that don't actually exist. If you feel that this may be a problem for you, do whatever you can to slow down during the test. Try taking a deep breath or counting to ten. As you read and consider the question, restrict yourself to the particular words used by the author. Avoid thought tangents about what the author *really* meant, or what he or she was *trying* to say. The only things that matter on a multiple-choice test are the words that are actually in the question. You must avoid reading too much into a multiple-choice question, or supposing that the writer meant something other than what he or she wrote.

5. No Need for Panic

It is wise to learn as many strategies as possible before taking a multiple-choice test, but it is likely that you will come across a few questions for which you simply don't know the answer. In this situation, avoid panicking. Because most multiple-choice tests include dozens of questions, the relative value of a single wrong answer is small. As much as possible, you should compartmentalize each question on a multiple-choice test. In other words, you should not allow your feelings about one question to affect your success on the others. When you find a question that you either don't understand or don't know how to answer, just take a deep breath and do your best. Read the entire question slowly and carefully. Try rephrasing the question a couple of different ways. Then, read all of the answer choices carefully. After eliminating obviously wrong answers, make a selection and move on to the next question.

6. Confusing Answer Choices

When working on a difficult multiple-choice question, there may be a tendency to focus on the answer choices that are the easiest to understand. Many people, whether consciously or not, gravitate to the answer choices that require the least concentration, knowledge, and memory. This is a mistake. When you come across an answer choice that is confusing, you should give it extra attention. A question might be confusing because you do not know the subject matter to which it refers. If this is the case, don't eliminate the answer before you have affirmatively settled on another. When you come across an answer choice of this type, set it aside as you look at the remaining choices. If you can confidently assert that one of the other choices is correct, you can leave the confusing answer aside. Otherwise, you will need to take a moment to try to better understand the confusing answer choice. Rephrasing is one way to tease out the sense of a confusing answer choice.

7. Your First Instinct

Many people struggle with multiple-choice tests because they overthink the questions. If you have studied sufficiently for the test, you should be prepared to trust your first instinct once you have carefully and completely read the question and all of the answer choices. There is a great deal of research suggesting that the mind can come to the correct conclusion very quickly once it has obtained all of the relevant information. At times, it may seem to you as if your intuition is working faster even than your reasoning mind. This may in fact be true. The knowledge you obtain while studying may be retrieved from your subconscious before you have a chance to work out the associations that support it. Verify your instinct by working out the reasons that it should be trusted.

8. Key Words

Many test takers struggle with multiple-choice questions because they have poor reading comprehension skills. Quickly reading and understanding a multiple-choice question requires a mixture of skill and experience. To help with this, try jotting down a few key words and phrases on a piece of scrap paper. Doing this concentrates the process of reading and forces the mind to weigh the relative importance of the question's parts. In selecting words and phrases to write down, the test taker thinks about the question more deeply and carefully. This is especially true for multiple-choice questions that are preceded by a long prompt.

9. Subtle Negatives

One of the oldest tricks in the multiple-choice test writer's book is to subtly reverse the meaning of a question with a word like *not* or *except*. If you are not paying attention to each word in the question, you can easily be led astray by this trick. For instance, a common question format is, "Which of the following is…?" Obviously, if the question instead is, "Which of the following is not…?," then the answer will be quite different. Even worse, the test makers are aware of the potential for this mistake and will include one answer choice that would be correct if the question were not negated or reversed. A test taker who misses the reversal will find what he or she believes to be a correct answer and will be so confident that he or she will fail to reread the question and discover the original error. The only way to avoid this is to practice a wide variety of multiple-choice questions and to pay close attention to each and every word.

10. Reading Every Answer Choice

It may seem obvious, but you should always read every one of the answer choices! Too many test takers fall into the habit of scanning the question and assuming that they understand the question because they recognize a few key words. From there, they pick the first answer choice that answers the question they believe they have read. Test takers who read all of the answer choices might discover that one of the latter answer choices is actually *more* correct. Moreover, reading all of the answer choices can remind you of facts related to the question that can help you arrive at the correct answer. Sometimes, a misstatement or incorrect detail in one of the latter answer choices will trigger your memory of the subject and will enable you to find the right answer. Failing to read all of the answer choices is like not reading all of the items on a restaurant menu: you might miss out on the perfect choice.

11. Spot the Hedges

One of the keys to success on multiple-choice tests is paying close attention to every word. This is never truer than with words like almost, most, some, and sometimes. These words are called "hedges" because they indicate that a statement is not totally true or not true in every place and time. An absolute statement will contain no hedges, but in many subjects, the answers are not always straightforward or absolute. There are always exceptions to the rules in these subjects. For this reason, you should favor those multiple-choice questions that contain hedging language. The presence of qualifying words indicates that the author is taking special care with his or her words, which is certainly important when composing the right answer. After all, there are many ways to be wrong, but there is only one way to be right! For this reason, it is wise to avoid answers that are absolute when taking a multiple-choice test. An absolute answer is one that says things are either all one way or all another. They often include words like *every, always, best,* and *never.* If you are taking a multiple-choice test in a subject that doesn't lend itself to absolute answers, be on your guard if you see any of these words.

12. Long Answers

In many subject areas, the answers are not simple. As already mentioned, the right answer often requires hedges. Another common feature of the answers to a complex or subjective question are qualifying clauses, which are groups of words that subtly modify the meaning of the sentence. If the question or answer choice describes a rule to which there are exceptions or the subject matter is complicated, ambiguous, or confusing, the correct answer will require many words in order to be expressed clearly and accurately. In essence, you should not be deterred by answer choices that seem excessively long. Oftentimes, the author of the text will not be able to write the correct answer without offering some qualifications and modifications. Your job is to read the answer choices thoroughly and completely and to select the one that most accurately and precisely answers the question.

13. Restating to Understand

Sometimes, a question on a multiple-choice test is difficult not because of what it asks but because of how it is written. If this is the case, restate the question or answer choice in different words. This process serves a couple of important purposes. First, it forces you to concentrate on the core of the question. In order to rephrase the question accurately, you have to understand it well. Rephrasing the question will concentrate your mind on the key words and ideas. Second, it will present the information to your mind in a fresh way. This process may trigger your memory and render some useful scrap of information picked up while studying.

14. True Statements

Sometimes an answer choice will be true in itself, but it does not answer the question. This is one of the main reasons why it is essential to read the question carefully and completely before proceeding to the answer choices. Too often, test takers skip ahead to the answer choices and look for true statements. Having found one of these, they are content to select it without reference to the question above. Obviously, this provides an easy way for test makers to play tricks. The savvy test taker will always read the entire question before turning to the answer choices. Then, having settled on a correct answer choice, he or she will refer to the original question and ensure that the selected answer is relevant. The mistake of choosing a correct-but-irrelevant answer choice is especially common on questions related to specific pieces of objective knowledge. A prepared test taker will have a wealth of factual knowledge at his or her disposal, and should not be careless in its application.

15. No Patterns

One of the more dangerous ideas that circulates about multiple-choice tests is that the correct answers tend to fall into patterns. These erroneous ideas range from a belief that B and C are the most common right answers, to the idea that an unprepared test-taker should answer "A-B-A-C-A-D-A-B-A." It cannot be emphasized enough that pattern-seeking of this type is exactly the WRONG way to approach a multiple-choice test. To begin with, it is highly unlikely that the test maker will plot the correct answers according to some predetermined pattern. The questions are scrambled and delivered in a random order. Furthermore, even if the test maker was following a pattern in the assignation of correct answers, there is no reason why the test taker would know which pattern he or she was using. Any attempt to discern a pattern in the answer choices is a waste of time and a distraction from the real work of taking the test. A test taker would be much better served by extra preparation before the test than by reliance on a pattern in the answers.

FREE DVD OFFER

Don't forget that doing well on your exam includes both understanding the test content and understanding how to use what you know to do well on the test. We offer a completely FREE Test Taking Tips DVD that covers world class test taking tips that you can use to be even more successful when you are taking your test.

All that we ask is that you email us your feedback about your study guide. To get your **FREE Test Taking Tips DVD**, email freedvd@studyguideteam.com with "FREE DVD" in the subject line and the following information in the body of the email:

- The title of your study guide.
- Your product rating on a scale of 1-5, with 5 being the highest rating.
- Your feedback about the study guide. What did you think of it?
- Your full name and shipping address to send your free DVD.

Introduction to the Praxis Reading Specialist (5301)

Function of the Test

The Praxis Reading Specialist test (5301), one of the Praxis Subject Assessments, is mainly intended for individuals with a graduate degree and who are interested in a career or position instructing or supervising the teaching of reading to students in grades K–12. The most successful test takers have a master's degree or comparable advanced education. The Praxis Reading Specialist test is most appropriate for candidates seeking a position with specialized responsibilities geared to the teaching of reading or supervising instructors who teach reading to students at any level in the K-12 range. Such positions might include reading instructors, supervisors, specialists, clinicians, consultants, supervisors, specialists, or coordinators.

Test Administration

The Praxis Reading Specialist test (5301) is administered via a computer-based format at Prometric testing centers around the country. It is offered during select two-week windows throughout a given year; the specific dates of administration are available on the website (https://www.ets.org/praxis/register/dates_centers/). Test takers who are not satisfied with their performance must wait at least 21 days before retaking the exam.

Individuals with documented disabilities who demonstrate a need can request accommodations for test administration. Requests can be completed online, or via mail or email. It is important to note that any test taker seeking accommodations is required to submit his or her request and receive approval back from ETS Disability Services prior to registering for the exam. The process of reviewing documentation and determining suitable accommodations takes approximately six weeks, so test takers should budget for this time.

Test Format

The Praxis Reading Specialist test (5301) lasts two hours and consists of two parts: Part A and Part B. Part A contains 80 multiple-choice questions (termed selective-response questions) and Part B entails one constructed-response question and one case study. The following table shows the breakdown of the sections and topics on the test:

Content Category	Approximate Number of Questions	Approximate Percentage of the Test
Part A: Multiple-Choice Questions	80	80%
Assessment and Diagnostic Teaching	20	20%
Reading and Writing Development	45	45%
Leadership Skills and Specialized Knowledge of Pedagogical Principles and Instructional Practices	15	15%
Part B: Constructed-Response Questions	2	20%
Professional Learning and Leadership	1	10%
Analysis of Individual Student Case Study	1	10%

Parts A and B are not independently timed, so test takers can partition their testing time as they please. With that said, it is recommended that 80 minutes are spent on Part A and 40 minutes are dedicated to Part B.

Scoring

Scores on the Praxis Reading Specialist exam range from 100-200. Scores are only based on the number of correct answers, so there is no penalty for guessing. In recent years, the median score has been 183. The passing score is determined by each state, so test takers should review the expectations of the state in which they are seeking a position.

Assessment and Diagnostic Teaching

Assessing Language Proficiency and Reading Skills

Oral and Written Language Proficiency

Formal and Informal Assessments
Formal assessments, such as selected-response questions, are a useful and quick way to grade students as opposed to free response assessments. However, **informal assessments** are an even quicker and more frequently used method of assessing students. Informal assessments can be conducted after a modeled lesson and before independent practice. The use of individual whiteboards and a few quick selected-response questions prepared before the lesson is a helpful tactic for teachers to quickly survey which students grasped the concepts and which students need additional reinforcement. Those who still need to master the skill can then be efficiently identified and grouped together for a small reteach.

Demonstrating Ability to Interpret Results
When using the results from formal assessments addressing multiple skills, it is important to group students according to ability for the particular skill of interest from the assessment and not just on the overall score. However, the overall score may be beneficial for grouping with regards to pacing and complexity of questions.

Results of Assessments
Grouping students should be continuous and change daily, or at least weekly. Each student's needs change from concept to concept. Assessments must be ongoing and frequent. Results from these ongoing assessments should be the driving force behind the grouping of students. Lessons and groups should be adjusted to the needs of the students.

Emergent Readers' Skills

Entry-level assessments, progress monitoring, and summative assessments need to be administered in order to determine students' print awareness, letter recognition, and alphabetic principle knowledge to identify misconceptions that can be remediated in future lessons. Formal and informal assessment methods are as follows:

- **Print awareness** is easily assessed through observation. Teachers can give students a book and ask them to demonstrate their tracking and orientation knowledge. Similarly, teachers can ask students to identify parts of a book, such as its title or page numbers.

- The **Concepts About Print (CAP) test** assesses a student's print awareness. The CAP test is administered one-on-one, typically at the beginning and middle of a student's kindergarten year. During the CAP test, the teacher asks a student questions about a book's print. The teacher records the student's responses to the questions asked on a standardized rubric. This helps to identify specific areas of weakness for each student in terms of print awareness. These areas can then be reinforced and retaught in future lessons.

Planned Observations

"**The Observation Survey**" created by Marie Clay, can be beneficial in the assessment of a student's letter recognition and alphabetic principle knowledge. The Observation Survey includes six literacy tasks:

1. Letter Identification
2. Concepts About Print
3. Writing Vocabulary
4. Hearing and Recording Sounds in Words
5. Text Reading
6. Word Test

Observation Study

During such assessments, a student may be asked to identify a letter's name, its sound, rhyming pairs, isolated initial/final phonemes, blending of compound words/syllables, and word segments, or to add or delete phonemes in words. Similarly, teachers can say a letter and ask students to write that letter on a sheet of paper. The teacher records student responses. In this way, the teacher can identify the skills that have not yet been mastered by a single student, small group, or entire class. The teacher can then use any of the aforementioned strategies to reinforce those skills within individuals, small groups, or whole-class instruction.

Ongoing Development of Reading Skills and Strategies

Letter-Sound Assessments

During phoneme and letter-sound correspondence assessments, teachers point to random letters or phonemes. The student is to then say the sound of the letter or phoneme and the teacher records the student's responses. Letter-sound combinations and phonemes with which a student, group, or class needs additional instruction and/or practice can be identified. The teacher can use this information to create lessons that emphasize the identified letter-sound correspondences and/or phonemes.

Phonics Assessments

Examples to test a student's ability to decode words or readily read sight words include Sylvia Green's Informal Word Analysis Inventory, Test of Word Reading Efficacy (TOWRE), and the CORE Phonics Survey. In these types of assessments, students are given a list of words and/or phonics patterns. Initially, high-frequency words that follow predictable phonics patterns are presented. Examples of **predictable phonics patterns** may include blending, word patterns, digraphs, etc. The words presented become more challenging as a student masters less difficult words. For example, a child may be assessed on his or her ability to decode nonsense words. The nonsense word assessments progress from decoding common sounds to less common sounds. Multisyllabic words within the assessments can reveal how well learners can chunk word parts through syllabication. As with other assessments discussed, the student's responses are recorded on a teacher's record sheet. In this way, the teacher can identify which word analysis principles and sight words a single student, a group of students, or an entire class is having difficulty with. These sight words, word parts, letter combinations, blending patterns, and/or syllabication principles can then be reinforced, retaught, reviewed, and practiced in future lessons. Additionally, the results of the assessment can be used to form instructional groups.

Informal Word Analysis Inventories   *encoding=spelling*

These can be used to assess encoding (spelling) of single-syllable words in the traditional manner. Students write the words that are read aloud by their teacher on a sheet of paper. In the early stages of spelling development, students are assessed on lists of words that are common to everyday language, share a word pattern or theme, and/or follow common orthographic patterns. The word lists become more complex as students demonstrate proficiency. The teacher can then plan instruction that targets the letter combinations and spelling patterns with which students are struggling. Such assessments can also be used to form instructional groups of students who share the same approximate developmental stage of spelling to better facilitate differentiated instruction.

As a general rule of thumb, isolated phonics tests should be given every four to six weeks. Spelling assessments can be given weekly or biweekly. Remediation should be implemented when students miss two or more questions on a five-question assessment and three or more questions on a ten-question assessment.

Contextualized Decoding Assessments

Despite the popularity of isolated decoding assessments, decoding should also be assessed in context. The **Word Recognition in Context** subtest of the Phonological Awareness Literacy Screening (PALS) is an example of an assessment that can be used for this purpose. During such assessments, passages that can be read by a student with 90% to 97% accuracy at acceptable rates are selected. The student reads these passages aloud to the teacher. By analyzing students' approaches to figuring out unknown words and students' errors when reading a grade-appropriate passage, teachers are better able to determine which of the following three decoding strategies to emphasize during instruction:

1. **Meaning cues** should be emphasized when a student fails to use context, story background, or pictures to assist in the decoding of new words.

2. **Structural cues** are emphasized when a student does not use grammar or syntax to figure out an unknown word.

3. **Visual cues** are emphasized when a student does not use grapheme or phoneme information to decode an unknown word. For example, a student may only read the beginning, middle, or end of words correctly (e.g., read hat as cat). A student may leave off a suffix or use incorrect yet similar letter combinations, indicating that visual cues need to be retaught.

Spelling Assessments

↳of words (not pictures)

Similarly, spelling should be assessed within the context of a student's writing samples. When a student's spelling is assessed in the context of a writing assignment, a teacher is able to detect patterns of misconceptions and areas that need remediation. Not only can such assessments be used to detect the proper encoding of words, but also a student's vocabulary, diction, and syntax. By using a rubric, teachers are better able to determine which developmental stage of spelling (the pre-phonetic stage, the semiphonetic stage, the phonetic stage, the transitional stage, and the conventional stage) of each student. Spelling instruction that targets each student's individual strengths, weaknesses, and developmental stage of spelling can then be created and implemented by the teacher.

Please note that once a student's areas of need are determined, any of the previously suggested phonics, sight word, and/or spelling strategies can be used for remediation and/or re-teaching of the identified skills.

Assessment Data

Methods of Assessment Data

Assessments are useful for identifying which students may be struggling with certain criteria as well as the specific areas of difficulty. Assessments can also indicate how well the material is being presented or provide vital clues on how to modify an individual student's instruction to help them grasp the content better. Generally, two types of assessments are used: informal and formal.

Informal assessments are not planned and lack a typical format or timeline. They can be as simple as watching and listening to how the students respond to answers in class or perform classwork. Observation is key. The instructor should be perceptive to how students not only respond to reading and language concepts but also to how they are interpreting them. If a student isn't understanding something such as a cultural reading concept, it may indicate that a more in-depth explanation is required. This will help the teacher adapt the instruction to enable the student to self-correct his or her own performance.

Formal assessments are partially based on observation, but are planned and implemented with the design to see how students respond to specific stimuli. They give a clearer indication of where students' weaknesses lie or whether they are on point in grasping the material. There are two primary methods for conducting formal assessments. The most conventional is a simple pencil-and-paper test in which students read prewritten questions and respond to them in writing. These physical answers provide a direct window into what the students know and how their reading comprehension is progressing. **Performance assessments** are a little less concrete but can provide a lot of insight into the student's mind-set and reactions that are more three-dimensional than a written assessment. This method does not use written responses, but instead analyzes students' performance in response to reading questions or activities. When giving performance assessments, it's important to bear in mind key questions: Does the student understand what they just read, did they seem uncomfortable when presenting their answer, and how accurate was their response? From here, new teaching strategies can be implemented, or the instructor can identify ways to provide specialized assistance to boost students' skills.

Diagnostic Reading Data to Accelerate Reading Skills

Whether an instructor uses informal or formal assessment, **data** will be produced from the assessment. This data, both written or gained through observation, is highly valuable in diagnosing whether to change teaching methods in order to accelerate students' reading skills development. Data-driven instruction guides reading improvement for all students simply because the data provides clear indications of where students are facing reading challenges or demonstrating strengths.

Differentiated instruction acknowledges that, while a group of students may be learning the same subject, the way each student learns and processes the subject is different. This technique looks at the different learning methods and reading areas that students respond best to in order to effect change. Therefore, an educator can then tailor, or differentiate, lessons to build on these skills and expedite the learning process. Differentiated instruction is divided into interest-based and ability-based instruction.

Much of a student's performance is based on their interest in the subject at hand. Sometimes a student may show difficulty reading because he or she isn't engaged in the material. One way to encourage reading growth is to allow students to choose their learning activities. This will give students ownership over their own education, enabling them to have fun while learning and to use specific activities they feel help them improve their reading abilities. For example, students more interested in visual activities may find reading more beneficial than listening to oral reading exercises.

Ability-based differentiation focuses on three core focus areas that determine reading proficiency and build skill. The first area of focus examines students' conceptual understanding of reading. If a teacher uses vocabulary or reading comprehension exercises in class, they will be able to examine how students are performing and modify instruction to address any confusion. This can also indicate students' preferences as well. The second differentiation looks at how students analyze and use the reading. Instructors must look at how students respond to questions and whether their interpretation is accurate. The final differentiation looks at how students evaluate and perform reading, creating a reaction that responds to the reading. The third differentiation looks at interpretation with the added step of using this knowledge to write or say something without being prompted that involves the reading. Identifying issues in one of these areas will narrow down where more emphasis must be placed to improve reading skills. Each reading area will affect the other two; improving one differentiated area will impact the others.

Diagnostic Reading Data for Reading Difficulties

Depending on where diagnostic data indicates areas of students' difficulty, reteaching certain material is a promising starting point to help students overcome their reading issues. This isn't a step backward in instruction; it's an alteration. Differentiated instruction offers opportunities for students to relearn reading principles in ways that best fit them individually.

If students are having reading difficulties, the lessons can be modified to be clearer or address the specific areas of difficulty. Sometimes, this means teaching the material in a different way entirely. Recalling the areas of differentiated instruction, there are many components of reading skills and understanding. If a student is having difficulty in one area, such as reading analysis, building on his or her conceptual knowledge and performance/evaluation reading skills could help connect the gaps in his or her analysis. For example, instead of just reading and responding to questions, students might grasp the material better through the use of simple logic. Breaking down sentence context and discussing the reading, rather than just asking questions and giving answers, can help bridge the gap in understanding, thus allowing students to draw further insight from the reading.

Considering what kind of activities improve which aspects of reading is also important. If students have phonetic problems, instructors should introduce activities that analyze the different aspects of words, as well as sounding out words, to build familiarity with English vocabulary and structure. To strengthen reading comprehension, incorporating activities that help students visualize what they read will help. Instructors should encourage students to paraphrase and summarize texts to examine their strengths and weaknesses as well. This will help the instructor identify what kind of differentiation may be necessary. Instead of shying away from challenging areas, it's important to modify lessons to help students approach the material with better focus and a renewed interest.

Student engagement will be instrumental in improving reading skills. Again, differential instruction encourages not only differentiated lessons and activities based on student ability, but also on interest. Having students design their own reading activities allows them to expand their skill sets while becoming eager to learn more. Activities such as synonym association for vocabulary words or even physically drawing out a given sentence will engage reading comprehension, analysis, and replication skills. Further assessments should be done to gauge the effectiveness of the new instruction methods.

Flexible Groupings for Changing Reading Needs

Another way to differentiate instruction is the use of groups and collaboration in going over or learning the reading material. In class, there are two forms of grouping instruction: teacher-based and student-based. A well-balanced and flexible learning environment will incorporate both types of grouping exercises to help students approach reading from multiple angles and practice problem-solving and critical-thinking skills. Students also strengthen social skills through flexible grouping.

Teacher-based grouping is organized by the instructor. This is the best method for introducing students to new material and exploring key concepts. Instructors may also choose to break the class up into small groups to provide instruction and work with students individually while the class is working. The goal here is to monitor students directly and provide differentiated instruction when necessary. This is the more variable of the two groupings and provides a more direct line for teacher intervention. However, students can also grasp concepts by interacting with their peers.

Student-based grouping focuses on students dictating the way the group is formed, essentially freeing the teacher to observe how they are interacting with others and approaching reading topics. Students can be given the option to form their groups independently or simply opening the class to a group discussion. This is different from actually lecturing because it allows students to talk about the reading subject among themselves as opposed to just listening and learning from the instructor. Posing questions for the class is a great way for students to learn correct answers and ask questions through simple conversation. Student-based groups are also excellent for school projects, allowing group members to pool their knowledge for success.

Flexible grouping relies on utilizing both teacher-based and student-based groupings throughout the instructional period. Using one more than the other isn't necessarily unbalanced, but the instructor should try to incorporate both groupings in order to broaden the students' experience. The teacher's choice in using either method should also relate to how they are implementing differentiated teaching methods. Educators can combine the use of grouping to suit activities and lessons for all areas in which students may be facing difficulties in order to boost confidence and clarify material.

Practice Questions

1. In the word *shul*, the *sh* is an example of what?
   a. Consonant digraph
   b. Sound segmentation
   c. Vowel digraph
   d. Rime

2. When students identify the phonemes in spoken words, they are practicing which of the following?
   a. Sound blending
   b. Substitution
   c. Rhyming
   d. Segmentation

3. What is the alphabetic principle?
   a. The understanding that letters represent sounds in words.
   b. The ability to combine letters to correctly spell words.
   c. The proper use of punctuation within writing.
   d. The memorization of all the letters in the alphabet.

4. Print awareness includes all EXCEPT which of the following concepts?
   a. The differentiation of uppercase and lowercase letters
   b. The identification of word boundaries
   c. The proper tracking of words
   d. The spelling of sight words

5. When teachers point to words during shared readings, what are they modeling?
   I. Word boundaries
   II. Directionality
   III. One-to-one correspondence
   a. I and II
   b. I and III
   c. II and III
   d. I, II, and III

6. Structural analysis would be the most appropriate strategy in determining the meaning of which of the following words?
   a. Extra
   b. Improbable
   c. Likely
   d. Wonder

7. A student spells *eagle* as *EGL*. This student is performing at which stage of spelling?
   a. Conventional
   b. Phonetic
   c. Semiphonetic
   d. Transitional

8. Spelling instruction should include which of the following?

    I. Word walls

    II. Daily reading opportunities

    III. Daily writing opportunities

    IV. Weekly spelling inventories with words students have studied during the week

  a. I and IV

  b. I, II, and III

  c. I, II, and IV

  d. I, II, III, and IV

9. A kindergarten student is having difficulty distinguishing the letters *b* and *d*. The teacher should do which of the following?

  a. Have the student use a think-aloud to verbalize the directions of the shapes used when writing each letter.

  b. Have the student identify the letters within grade-appropriate texts.

  c. Have the student write each letter five times.

  d. Have the student write a sentence in which all of the letters start with either *b* or *d*.

10. When differentiating phonics instruction for English-language learners (ELLs), teachers should do which of the following?

  a. Increase the rate of instruction

  b. Begin with the identification of word boundaries

  c. Focus on syllabication

  d. Capitalize on the transfer of relevant skills from the learners' original language(s)

11. Which of the following is the most appropriate assessment of spelling for students who are performing at the pre-phonetic stage?

  a. Sight word drills

  b. Phonemic awareness tests

  c. Writing samples

  d. Concepts about print (CAP) test

12. Phonological awareness is best assessed through which of the following?

  a. Identification of rimes or onsets within words

  b. Identification of letter-sound correspondences

  c. Comprehension of an audio book

  d. Writing samples

13. The identification of morphemes within words occurs during the instruction of what?

  a. Structural analysis

  b. Syllabic analysis

  c. Phonics

  d. The alphabetic principle

14. Which of the following pairs of words are homophones?

  a. Playful and replay

  b. To and too

  c. Was and were

  d. Gloomy and sad

15. Nursery rhymes are used in kindergarten to develop what?
    a. Print awareness
    b. Phoneme recognition
    c. Syllabication
    d. Structural analysis

16. High-frequency words such as *be, the*, and *or* are taught during the instruction of what?
    a. Phonics skills
    b. Sight word recognition
    c. Vocabulary development
    d. Structural analysis

17. To thoroughly assess students' phonics skills, teachers should administer assessments that require students to do which of the following?
    a. Decode in context only
    b. Decode in isolation only
    c. Both A and B
    d. Neither A nor B

18. A student is having difficulty pronouncing a word that she comes across when reading aloud. Which of the following is most likely NOT a reason for the difficulty that the student is experiencing?
    a. Poor word recognition
    b. A lack of content vocabulary
    c. Inadequate background knowledge
    d. Repeated readings

19. Which is the largest contributor to the development of students' written vocabulary?
    a. Reading
    b. Directed reading
    c. Direct teaching
    d. Modeling

20. The study of roots, suffixes, and prefixes is called what?
    a. Listening comprehension
    b. Word consciousness
    c. Word morphology
    d. Textual analysis

Answer Explanations

1. A: The *sh* is an example of a consonant digraph. Consonant diagraphs are combinations of two or three combinations of consonants that work together to make a single sound. Examples of consonant digraphs are *sh*, *ch*, and *th*. Choice *B*, sound segmentation, is used to identify component phonemes in a word, such as separating the /t/, /u/, and /b/ for *tub*. Choice *C*, vowel digraph, are sets of two vowels that make up a single sound, such as *ow*, *ae*, or *ie*. Choice *D*, rime, is the sound that follows a word's onset, such as the /at/ in *cat*.

2. D: Sound segmentation is the identification of all the component phonemes in a word. An example would be the student identifying each separate sound, /t/, /u/, and /b/, in the word *tub*. Choice *A*, sound blending, is the blending together of two or more sounds in a word, such as /ch/ or /sh/. Choice *B*, substitution, occurs when a phoneme is substituted within a word for another phoneme, such as substituting the sound /b/ in *bun* to /r/ to create *run*. Choice *C*, rhyming, is an effective tool to utilize during the analytic phase of phonics development because rhyming words are often identical except for their beginning letters.

3. A: The alphabetical principle is the understanding that letters represent sounds in words. It is through the alphabetic principle that students learn the interrelationships between letter-sound (grapheme-phoneme) correspondences, phonemic awareness, and early decoding skills (such as sounding out and blending letter sounds).

4. D: Print awareness includes all except the spelling of sight words. Print awareness includes Choice *A*, the differentiation of uppercase and lowercase letters, so that students can understand which words begin a sentence. Choice *B*, the identification of word boundaries, is also included in print awareness; that is, students should be made aware that words are made up of letters and that spaces appear between words, etc. Choice *C*, the proper tracking of words, is also included in print awareness; this is the realization that print is organized in a particular way, so books must be tracked and held accordingly.

5. D: Word boundaries is included as one of the factors modeled because students should be able to identify which letters make up a word as well as the spaces before and after the letters that make up words. Directionality is the ability to track words as they are being read, so this is also modeled. One-to-one correspondence, the last factor listed, is the ability to match written letters to words to a spoken word when reading. It is another thing teachers model when they point to words while they read.

6. B: Structural analysis focuses on the meaning of morphemes. Morphemes include base words, prefixes, and word endings (inflections and suffixes) that are found within longer words. Students can use structural analysis skill to find familiar word parts within an unfamiliar word in order to decode the word and determine the definition of the new word. The prefix im- (meaning not) in the word "improbable" can help students derive the definition of an event that is not likely to occur.

7. B: The student is performing at the phonetic stage. Phonetic spellers will spell a word as it sounds. The speller perceives and represents all of the phonemes in a word. However, because phonetic spellers have limited sight word vocabulary, irregular words are often spelled incorrectly.

8. B: The creation of word walls, Choice *I*, is advantageous during the phonetic stage of spelling development. On a word wall, words that share common consonant-vowel patterns or letter clusters are written in groups. Choices *II* and *III*, daily reading and writing opportunities, are also important in spelling instructions. Students need daily opportunities in order to review and practice spelling development. Daily journals or exit tickets are cognitive writing strategies effective in helping students reflect on what they have learned. A spelling inventory, Choice *IV*, is different than a traditional spelling test because students are not allowed to study the words prior to the administration of a spelling inventory. Therefore, this option is incorrect as it mentions the inventory contains words students have studied all week.

9. A: The teacher should have the student use a think-aloud to verbalize the directions of the shapes used when writing each letter. During think-alouds, teachers voice the metacognitive process that occurs when writing each part of a given letter. Students should be encouraged to do likewise when practicing writing the letters.

10. D: Teachers should capitalize on the transfer of relevant skills from the learner's original language(s). In this way, extra attention and instructional emphasis can be applied toward the teaching of sounds and meanings of words that are nontransferable between the two languages.

11. C: Writing sample are the most appropriate assessment of spelling for students who are performing at the pre-phonetic stage s. During the pre-phonetic stage, students participate in precommunicative writing. Precommunicative writing appears to be a jumble of letter-like forms rather than a series of discrete letters. Samples of students' precommunicative writing can be used to assess their understanding of the alphabetic principle and their knowledge of letter-sound correspondences.

12. A: Phonological awareness is best assessed through identification of rimes or onsets within words. Instruction of phonological awareness includes detecting and identifying word boundaries, syllables, onset/rime, and rhyming words.

13. A: The identification of morphemes within words occurs during the instruction of structural analysis. Structural analysis is a word recognition skill that focuses on the meaning of word parts, or morphemes, during the introduction of a new word. Choice *B*, syllabic analysis, is a word analysis skill that helps students split words into syllables. Choice *C*, phonics, is the direct correspondence between and blending of letters and sounds. Choice *D*, the alphabetic principle, teaches that letters or other characters represent sounds.

14. B: Homophones are words that are pronounced the same way but differ in meaning and/or spelling. The pair *to* and *too* is an example of a homophone because they are pronounced the same way, but differ in both meaning and spelling. Choices *A*, *C*, and *D* are not homophones because they do not sound the same when spoken aloud.

15. B: Nursery rhymes are used in kindergarten to develop phoneme recognition. Rhyming words are often almost identical except for their beginning letter(s), so rhyming is a great strategy to implement during the analytic phase of phoneme development.

16. B: High-frequency words are taught during the instruction of sight word recognition. Sight words, sometimes referred to as high-frequency words, are words that are used often but may not follow the regular principles of phonics. Sight words may also be defined as words that students are able to recognize and read without having to sound out.

17. C: Both *A* and *B*. Decoding should be assessed in context in addition to isolation. During such assessments, the students read passages from reading-level appropriate texts aloud to the teacher so that the teacher is better able to analyze a student's approach to figuring out unknown words. Decoding should also be assessed in isolation. In these types of assessments, students are given a list of words and/or phonics patterns. Initially, high-frequency words that follow predictable phonics patterns are presented. The words that are presented become more challenging as a student masters less difficult words.

18. D: An individual's sight vocabulary includes the words that he or she can recognize and correctly pronounce when reading. Limited sight vocabulary can be caused by poor word recognition, a lack of content vocabulary, and inadequate background knowledge. Although proper pronunciation may affect the ability to spell a word, the ability to properly spell a word is less likely to affect a student's ability to properly pronounce that word.

19. A: There is a positive correlation between a student's exposure to text and the academic achievement of that individual. Therefore, students should be given ample opportunities to read independently as much text as possible in order to gain vocabulary and background knowledge.

20. C: By definition, morphology is the identification and use of morphemes such as root words and affixes. Listening comprehension refers to the processes involved in understanding spoken language. Word consciousness refers to the knowledge required for students to learn and effectively utilize language. Textual analysis is an approach that researchers use to gain information and describe the characteristics of a recorded or visual message.

Reading and Writing Development

Oral Language and Communication Skills

Instructional Strategies for Oral Language, Listening and Speaking Skills, and Vocabularies

Oral Language
Oral or spoken language is also important when understanding a text. If proficient, a reader's speech will aid his or her ability to understand and comprehend words, sentences, paragraphs, and a variety of complex texts.

Listening Comprehension and Oral Language Activities
Oral language activities, such as purposeful read-alouds, allow students to focus on comprehension skills. Listening skills can promote and serve as a great foundation for comprehension skills. Understanding a text advances students' comprehension skills. When an instructor reads aloud, a student does not need to decode words for fluency. This allows students to listen and focus solely on the text for comprehension. Teacher read-alouds also provide students the opportunity to learn how to emphasize voice and tone while reading.

Building Oral Communication Skills

Oral language and presentation are also important in learning reading comprehension. Reviewing and identifying new and key vocabulary prior to reading the text helps students understand the text more efficiently. Once students are familiar with new vocabulary words, they will understand the paragraph with a new key word when approaching it, rather than reaching the word and skipping over the true meaning of the sentence or paragraph at large, or needing to stop and look up the word before continuing to read. This interrupts fluency as well as the understanding of text. Previewing text and skimming pictures for younger students, or reviewing bold subtitles for older students, can benefit students' comprehension by helping to gain an idea of what the text may be about before reading. There are different ways to find a text's purpose using auditory and speech skills, some of which include summarizing with a peer or paraphrasing the text.

When students are paired together or placed in small groups, they can share and discuss elements of texts. Literature circles are like book clubs. These circles allow students to speak freely, create their own discussions, and form questions about the text. Teachers can provide literature circle booklets, which may contain response or discussion questions to enhance conversation within the group.

Oral and Nonverbal Communication Skills in Various Settings

Early childhood educators are instrumental in developing effective communication skills in their students. Verbal and nonverbal communication skills are important in setting a positive, educational, supportive environment to optimize learning. They are equally important for students to master for use in their own daily lives. When communicating with others, students should be mindful to be fully attentive, make eye contact, and use encouraging facial expressions and body language to augment positive verbal feedback. Postures including hands on hips or crossed over the chest may appear standoffish, while smiling and nodding enhance the comfort and satisfaction of the other party. Active listening is the process of trying to understand the underlying meaning in someone else's words, which builds empathy and trust. Asking open-ended questions and repeating or rephrasing in a reflective or clarifying manner is a form of active listening that builds a positive, trusting relationship.

In tandem with different communication styles, educators and students alike should be aware of different learning styles. **Auditory learners** learn through hearing, so the educator can use verbal descriptions and instructions. **Visual learners** learn through observation, so the educator can use demonstrations, provide written and pictorial instructional content, and show videos. **Kinesthetic learners** learn through movement, involvement, and experience, so the educator can prepare lessons with hands-on learning, labs, or games with a physical component.

An important skill for children is the ability to communicate effectively with adults, and developing this comfort from a young age will be helpful throughout life. Educators can facilitate this through providing experiences where children need to talk to adults in the community. For example, educators may take the class on a field trip to the local community library, where students must ask the librarian for help locating certain health resources. Students might also prepare a health fair and invite parents, community members, and those from senior centers to come learn from posters, demonstrations, and presentations. Children can also work on developing communication skills using an array of technologies such as telephone, written word, email, and face-to-face communication.

Oral Language Structures

Oral language skills are important for students to have in order to thrive in an English-speaking environment. Beyond comprehending spoken English, understanding oral language structure helps students comprehend the context of what they are reading and how to respond appropriately. All languages utilize grammar, vocabulary, phonology, morphology, discourse, and pragmatics; these concepts combine to make words on a page actually form communication—the foundation of sentences.

As an instructor, it's important to be mindful of how comfortable the class is with oral language. Native speakers may be more proficient than those who are learning English as a second language; the latter may need more differentiated instruction to build their conceptual knowledge. No matter the range of student experiences, reading instructors should incorporate drills and lessons that frequently review oral language components throughout the course. This will ensure that core skills such as grammar and word formation remain fresh in students' minds as they continue to progress in reading proficiency. This can be done in a variety of ways and activities using both teacher-based and student-based grouping instruction.

Strategically, it's best to promote oral language by having students isolate and identify different aspects of sentences such as grammar and even vocabulary terms. Reviewing **phonology**, the sounds of English, and **morphology**, how words are formed, is also important. One way to review these aspects would be to present a sample of text and then have students deconstruct the sentences to identify these structures.

Discourse, which studies how language is used in communication, and **pragmatics**, which reflects the correct use of the language, can be reviewed through text examination and interactive activities. It's important to alter and differentiate instruction to review reading principles in different ways and expand critical-thinking skills. One method for reviewing discourse and pragmatics would be for the instructor to write or speak a sentence and then have the class discuss the discourse and pragmatics together. Students can also create the sentences themselves, demonstrating their ability to replicate correct language structure and recognize incorrect sentence components. When reviewing language structure, instructors should continue to assess how students are grasping the material and monitor progress. It's important to remember that reading improvements begin with a strong understanding of language fundamentals.

Learning of Standard American English by Speakers of Other Languages

Inevitably, all languages deviate from their standard format. In America, Standard American English has evolved into different forms (**dialects**) that are spoken across the country based on cultural influences and location. These dialects, while still considered English, are not Standard English. This is because some of the grammar, pronunciations, or general phonetics are inconsistent with the designated standard. Whether students are native English speakers or learning English as a second language, learning Standard English will give them a holistic understanding of American language conventions.

Students have likely encountered examples of American English deviation before, so the risk here is that they think slang or idiomatic choices reflect correct English usage. It's important to frequently review English language structure to ensure students know the proper pronunciations of words and how sentences fit together. However, this still doesn't eliminate confusion with hearing other English dialects; after all, these dialects are still English. One way to teach students Standard American English is to illustrate the difference between the standard and other dialects.

Citing specific examples of dialectic English that are incorrect from the standard is key. For example, Americans living in the South tend to use the word *y'all* to summarize the phrase *you all*. *Y'all* isn't recognized as part of Standard American English, so the correct version is *you all*. Distinctions such as this will help students visualize and hear proper English in use, which will help them recognize and use Standard English when reading and speaking.

In addition to reviewing proper word use and phonetics, training should also incorporate pronunciation. Writing and reading Standard English is very important, but students should also be knowledgeable of the incorrect and correct way to say the words they're reading. In addition to explaining pronunciation rules, instructors can periodically ask students to say and pronounce random words in a reading passage to test their skills. Again, showing students correct and incorrect pronunciations will build their familiarity with correct Standard English and help them distinguish wrong pronunciation tropes. Visualization activities and tools will also help. Flash cards with pronunciation guides for keywords are just one way to help students pronounce difficult vocabulary words.

Relationship Between Language Acquisition and Students with Disorders

The **Nativist theory of language development** holds that humans learn speech naturally as a result of inborn ability. According to the theory, children naturally have a language acquisition device that enables them to understand and eventually replicate the language. Children are naturally inclined to pick up language. However, this view can be seen as contrary to the **interactionist learning view**, which holds that children learn language as a result of their interaction with others. Therefore, the more children are exposed to language, the more they pick up vocabulary and can string together phrases. It's helpful and open-minded to consider that both ideas impact language learning.

An instructor can assess students to see if their issues are based on lack of instruction or erroneous exposure to language or if a student has a learning disorder that is inhibiting their ability to learn as fluidly as other students. There are several language-related disorders and delays that could be making reading difficult for students, so identifying these issues early is key.

Instructors must be patient and engaging to assess student performance and encourage them to not fear failure. Hearing how students respond to reading or actually speak will give indications of what issues are present. For example, students who face difficulties with written English by reversing words or letters and sometimes having trouble identifying rhyming words may have common **dyslexia**. Another common problem is difficulty recognizing letter sounds, which delays students' language progression. All of these issues may occur naturally, interrupting learning ability, but they can be treated through differentiated instruction.

The most effective way to remedy language issues is to identify specific areas of difficulties and provide supplemental instruction. This process is referred to as **articulation therapy**. The first step is isolation, to see if students can make key sounds or help them make the sounds needed for English. Instructors then work to improve the students' understanding of syllables, words, phrases, sentences, reading, and conversation. All of these areas build on each other. Improving English sound production will impact the understanding of syllables and words and therefore pave the way for reading and speaking proficiency.

Linguistic and Cultural Diversity

The classroom must be a place that emphasizes respect for all individuals as well as collaboration to achieve a successful learning environment. In addition to teaching reading skills, the instructor is expected to be a model of tolerance and inclusiveness for all students, thus encouraging them to be open-minded toward others. In the United States, it's likely that instructors will have students from a broad range of cultural and linguistic backgrounds. Obviously, these students must be made to feel welcome, and any linguistic difficulties they have should be treated as simply another step in the learning process, not a result of their background. Any difficulty is an opportunity for the whole class to learn and grow.

Encouraging polite and respectful behavior is key. An instructor doesn't necessarily need to explain polite behavior, but rather, should serve as a role model for the class. When addressing students' issues, the teacher should be sensitive to how they feel and be encouraging no matter their religious or ethnic background. It's also important to monitor how students act and respond to one another. Proper language and behavior should be enforced when necessary, and if there is ever anything rude or insensitive said or done, it must be addressed and corrected. Teachers should emphasize the idea that, while everyone is different, they are all equal. Therefore, students must be treated respectfully. Teachers should observe whether students are listening to other students and not being distracted or showing signs of disrespect. Tone and physical behavior must also be monitored; there's no excuse for rudeness. When disrespect occurs, steps should be taken to ensure it isn't repeated. It's important to remember that behaviors and lessons in early learners will inform how children grow and mature.

Reading and writing activities can also provide lessons in respect and collaboration. For instance, students can do group work on a text that discusses respectful behavior for reading practice, and also talk about the meaning of the written content. Other lessons can look at readings from different cultures to expand the students' appreciation and interest in diversity.

Phonological Awareness

Phonological Association Skills

Phonological Awareness vs. Phonemic Awareness
Phonological awareness is the recognition that oral language is made of smaller units, such as syllables and words. Phonemic awareness is a type of phonological awareness. Phonemic-aware students recognize specific units of spoken language called phonemes. **Phonemes** are unique and easily identifiable units of sound. Examples include /t/, /b/, /c/, etc. It is through phonemes that words are distinguished from one another.

Phonemic Awareness in Reading Development

Phonological and phonemic awareness do not require written language because phonemic awareness is based entirely upon speech. However, phonological and phonemic awareness are the prerequisites for literacy. Thus, experts recommend that all kindergarten students develop phonemic awareness as part of their reading preparation.

Once students are able to recognize phonemes of spoken language, phonics can be implemented in grades K-2. Phonics is the direct correspondence between and blending of letters and sounds. Unlike phonemic awareness, **phonics** requires the presence of print. Phonics often begins with the alphabetic principle, which teaches that letters or other characters represent sounds. Students must be able to identify letters, symbols, and individual sounds before they can blend multiple sounds into word parts and whole words. Thus, phoneme awareness and phonics predict outcomes in word consciousness, vocabulary, reading, and spelling development.

Types of Phonemic Awareness Skills

Instruction of phonological awareness includes detecting and identifying word boundaries, syllables, onset/rime, and rhyming words. Each of these skills is explained below.

1. **Word boundaries:** Students must be able to identify how many letters are in a word and that spaces between words indicate where a word begins and ends.

2. **Syllables:** A syllable is a unit of speech that contains a vowel sound. A syllable does not necessarily have to be surrounded by consonants. Therefore, every syllable has a rime. However, not every syllable has an onset.

3. **Onset:** An onset is the beginning sound of any word. For example, /c/ is the onset in the word cat.

4. **Rime:** The rime of a word is the sound that follows the word's onset. The /at/ is the rime in the word cat.

5. **Syllabification:** Syllabification is the dividing of words into their component syllables. Syllabification should begin with single-syllable words and progress toward multi-syllable words.

6. **Rhyming words:** Rhyming words are often almost identical except for their beginning letter(s). Therefore, rhyming is an effective strategy to implement during the analytic phase of phonics development.

Instruction of phonemic awareness includes recognizing, blending, segmenting, deleting, and substituting phonemes. These skills are explained below:

Phoneme Recognition

Phoneme recognition occurs when students recognize that words are made of separate sounds and they are able to distinguish the initial, middle, and final phonemes within words. Initial awareness of phonemes should be done in isolation and not within words. Then, phoneme awareness can be achieved through shared readings that are supplemented with identification activities, such as the identification of rhyming words.

Blending

Sound blending is the ability to mix together two or more sounds or phonemes. For example, a **consonant blend** is a combination of two or more consonants into a single sound such as /ch/ or /sh/. Blending often begins when the teacher models the slow pronunciation of sound parts within a word. Students are to do likewise, with scaffolding provided by the teacher. Eventually, the pronunciation rate is increased, so that the full word is spoken as it would be in normal conversation.

Segmenting

Sound segmentation is the ability to identify the component phonemes in a word. Segmentation begins with simple, single-syllable words. For instance, a teacher might pronounce the word tub and see if students can identify the /t/, /u/, and /b/ sounds. The student must identify all three sounds in order for sound segmentation to be complete.

Deleting

Sound deletion is an oral activity in which one of the phonemes of a spoken word is removed. For example, a teacher may say a word aloud and then ask students to say the word without a specific sound (e.g., "What word would be formed if cat is said without the /c/ sound?"). With repetition, deletion activities can improve phoneme recognition.

Substituting

Like deletion, **substitution** takes place orally and is initiated through modeling. However, instead of deleting a phoneme or syllable, spoken words are manipulated via the substitution of phonemes for others (e.g., "What word would be formed if we change the /b/ in bun to /r/?").

Hearing, Saying, and Manipulating Phonemes

Differentiating Instruction to Reach a Full Range of Learners
The following strategies can be used to develop phonological and phonemic awareness in students that struggle with reading, disabled learners, special-needs students, English Language Learners (ELLs), speakers of nonstandard English, and advanced learners:

- Differentiated instruction for struggling readers, disabled students, or students with special needs should include the re-teaching and/or emphasis of key skills, such as blending and segmenting. Such instruction should be supported through the employment of a variety of concrete examples that explain a concept or task. Teaching strategies of such concepts or tasks should utilize visual, kinesthetic, and tactile modalities, and ample practice time should be allotted.

- Instruction of phonological and phonemic awareness can also be differentiated for ELLs and speakers of nonstandard English. Most English phonemes are present in other languages.

Therefore, teachers can capitalize on the transfer of relevant knowledge, skills, and phonemes from a student's primary language into the English language. In this way, extra attention and instructional emphasis can be applied toward phonemes and phoneme sequences that are nontransferable between the two languages.

- Advanced learners benefit from phonological and phonemic instruction with greater breadth and depth. Such instruction should occur at a faster pace and expand students' current skills.

<u>Continual Assessment of Phonological and Phonemic Awareness Needs to Occur</u>
Entry-level assessments, progress monitoring, and summative assessments need to be administered in order to determine students' phonological and phonemic awareness. Appropriate formal and informal assessments for such purposes include:

The Yopp-Singer Test of Phonemic Segmentation
This is an oral entry-level or summative assessment of phonemic awareness during which a teacher reads one of twenty-two words aloud at a time to a single student. The student is to break each word apart by stating the word's sounds in the order that the sounds are heard or said, and the teacher records the student's responses. Correctly segmented letter sounds are circled and incorrect responses are noted. If a student does well, then he or she is likely to do well in other phonemic areas. Upon poor student performance, the sound(s) with which a student struggles should be emphasized and/or retaught shortly after the time of the assessment.

After the Yopp-Singer Test, the blending of words, syllabification, and/or onset-rime identification should be assessed. The last set of phonological and phonemic skills to be assessed is composed of isolation, blending, deletion, and substitution.

Recognizing Rhyme Assessment
Word awareness, specifically awareness of onset-rime, can be assessed as a progress-monitoring activity. During this assessment, the teacher says two words. Students are to point their thumbs up if the words rhyme and down if the words do not rhyme. Immediate feedback and remediation are provided if the majority of the students respond incorrectly to a word pair.

Isolation or Matching Games
Games can be used to identify initial, medial, and final phonemes. During a phoneme-isolation activity, the teacher says one word at a time. The student is to tell the teacher the first, medial, or last sound of the word. During phoneme-matching activities, a teacher reads a group of words. The student is to say which two words from the group begin or end with the same sound. A similar activity can be completed to assess deletion and/or substitution (e.g., "What word would result if we replaced the /c/ of *cat* with an *h*?"). In this way, teachers can assess if remediation or extra instruction on initial, medial, or final phonemes is required, and lessons can be developed accordingly.

Phoneme Blending Assessment
In this assessment, a teacher says all the sounds within a word and a student listens to the teacher and is asked for the word that they hear when the sounds are put together quickly. This skill will be needed when students learn letter-sound pairs and decipher unknown words in their reading. Thus, mastery of this assessment can be used as an indicator to the teacher that the students are ready to learn higher-level phonological and/or phonemic tasks.

Please note that student results should be recorded, analyzed, and used to determine if students demonstrate mastery over the assessed skill and/or identify the needs of students. If mastery is not demonstrated, then the assessments should be used to determine exactly which letter-sound combinations or other phonemes need to be remediated. Any of the strategies earlier addressed (rhyming, blending, segmenting, deleting, substituting) can be used for such purposes.

Concepts of Print and Basic Phonetic Principles

Concepts of Print and High-Frequency Sight Words

Print awareness aids reading development, as it is the understanding that the printed word represents the ideas voiced in spoken language. Print awareness includes the understanding that:

(word boundaries)

1. Words are made of letters; spaces appear between words and words make sentences.

2. Print is organized in a particular way (e.g., read from left to right and top to bottom, read from front to back, etc.), so books must be tracked and held accordingly.

3. There are different types of print for different purposes (magazines, billboards, essays, fiction, etc.).

Print awareness provides the foundation on which all other literacy skills are built. It is often the first stage of reading development. Without print awareness, a student is not likely to develop letter-sound correspondence, word reading skills, or reading comprehension skills. For this reason, a child's performance on tasks relevant to their print awareness is indicative of the child's future reading achievement.

The following strategies can be used to increase print awareness in students:

1. *An adult reads aloud to students and shared reading experiences*. In order to maximize print awareness within the student, the reader should point out the form, function, orientation, and sounds of letters and words.

2. *Shared readings also build one-to-one correspondence*. **One-to-one correspondence** is the ability to match written letters or words to a spoken word when reading. This can be accomplished by pointing to words as they are read. This helps students make text-to-word connections. Pointing also aids **directionality**, or the ability to track the words that are being read.

3. *Use the child's environment*. To reinforce print awareness, teachers can make a child aware of print in their environment, such as words on traffic signs. Teachers can reinforce this by labeling objects in the classroom.

4. *Instruction of book organization can occur during read-alouds*. Students should be taught the proper orientation, tracking, and numbering conventions of books. For example, teachers can differentiate the title from the author's name on the front cover of a book.

5. *Let students practice*. Allowing students to practice book-handling skills with wordless, predictable, or patterned text will help to instill print awareness.

Uppercase and Lowercase Letters

Among the skills that are used to determine reading readiness, letter identification is the strongest predictor. **Letter recognition** is the identification of each letter in the alphabet. Letter recognition does not include letter-sound correspondences; however, learning about and being able to recognize letters may increase student motivation to learn letter sounds. Also, the names of many letters are similar to their sounds, so letter recognition serves as a gateway for the letter-sound relationships that are needed for reading to occur. Similarly, the ability to differentiate between uppercase and lowercase letters is beneficial in determining where a sentence begins and ends.

To be fluent in letter identification, students should be able to identify letter names in and out of context with automaticity. In order to obtain such familiarity with the identification of letters, students need ample experience, acquaintance, and practice with letters. Explicit instruction in letter recognition, practice printing uppercase and lowercase letters of the alphabet, and consistent exposure to printed letters are essential in the instruction of letter recognition.

Research has revealed that the following sequencing guidelines are necessary to effectively promote letter naming and identification:

1. The initial stage includes visual discrimination of shapes and curved lines.

2. Once students are able to identify and discriminate shapes with ease, then letter formations can be introduced. During the introduction of letter shapes, two letters that share visual (*p* and *q*) or auditory (/a/ and /u/) similarities should never be presented in back-to-back.

3. Next, uppercase letters are introduced. Uppercase letters are introduced before lowercase letters because they are easier to discriminate visually than lowercase letters. When letter formations are first presented to a student, their visual system analyzes the vertical, horizontal, and curved orientations of the letters. Therefore, teachers should use think-alouds when instructing how to write the shape of each letter. During think-alouds, teachers verbalize their own thought processes that occur when writing each part of a given letter. Students should be encouraged to do likewise when practicing printing the letters.

4. Once uppercase letters are mastered, lowercase letters can be introduced. High-frequency lowercase letters (*a, e, t*) are introduced prior to low-frequency lowercase letters (*q, x, z*).

5. Once the recognition of letters is mastered, students need ample time manipulating and utilizing the letters. This can be done through sorting, matching, comparing, and writing activities.

Basic Phonetic Principles

The **alphabetic principle** is the understanding of the names and sounds produced by letters, letter patterns, and symbols printed on a page. Through the alphabetic principle, students learn letter-sound correspondence, phonemic awareness, and the application of simple decoding skills such as the sounding out and blending of letter sounds. Since reading is essentially the blending together of multiple letter sounds, the alphabetic principle is crucial in reading development.

As with the instruction of letter recognition, research has revealed the following sequence to be effective in the teaching of the alphabetic principle:

1. Letter-sound relationships need to be taught explicitly and in isolation. The rate at which new letter-sound correspondences can be presented will be unique to the student group. The order in which letters are presented should permit students to read words quickly. Therefore, letter-sound pairs that are used frequently should be presented before letter-sound pairs with lower utility. Similarly, it is suggested to first present consonant letter-sound pairs that can be pronounced in isolation without distortion (*f, m, s, r*). Instruction of letters that sound similar should not be presented in proximity.

2. Once single-letter and sound combinations are mastered, consonant blends and clusters (*br, ch, gr*) can be presented.

Invented Spellings and Phonetic Principles

When children begin to learn the various letter-sound correspondences, their phonemic awareness begins to overlap with their awareness of orthography and reading. One of the widely accepted strategies to employ when introducing children to letter-sound correspondences is to begin with those correspondences that occur the most frequently in simple English words. In an effort to help build confidence in young learners, educators are encouraged to introduce only a few letter-sound combinations at a time and provide ample opportunities for practice and review before introducing new combinations. Although there is no formally established order for the introduction of letter-sound correspondences, educators are encouraged to consider the following general guidelines, but they should also keep in mind the needs, experiences, and current literacy levels of the students. The following is intended as a general guide only:

1. a	6. n	11. g	16. l	21. x
2. m	7. c	12. h	17. e	22. v
3. t	8. d	13. i	18. r	23. y
4. p	9. u	14. f	19. w	24. z
5. o	10. s	15. b	20. k	25. j
				26. q

As a generally accepted rule, short vowels should be introduced ahead of long vowels, and lowercase letters should be mastered before the introduction of their upper case counterparts.

Spelling conventions in the English language are primarily concerned with three areas: mechanics, usage, and sentence formation.

Mechanics
For primary students who are just beginning to master the alphabetic principle, educators should first concentrate on proper letter formation, the spelling of high-frequency words and sight words, and offer classroom discussions to promote the sharing of ideas. When children begin to write in sentences to share their thoughts and feelings in print, educators may consider the introduction of an author's chair, in which students read their writing out loud to their classmates.

Although the phonetic spelling or invented spelling that primary students employ in these early stages may not be the conventional spelling of certain words, it allows primary students to practice the art and flow of writing. It works to build their confidence in the writing process. This is not the time for educators to correct spelling, punctuation, or capitalization errors, as young learners may quickly lose interest in writing and may lose self-confidence.

One strategy to employ early on to help students with proper spelling is to ensure there is an easily accessible and updated word wall that employs high-frequency words and sight words. Students should be encouraged to refer to the word wall while they write.

Usage

Usage concerns itself with word order, verb tense, and subject-verb agreement among other areas. As primary children often have a basic knowledge of how to use oral language effectively in order to communicate, this area of spelling conventions may require less initial attention than the mechanics of spelling. During read-aloud and shared reading activities, educators may wish to point out punctuation marks found in print, model how to read these punctuation marks, and periodically discuss their importance in the reading and writing process.

When children begin to engage in writing exercises, educators may wish to prompt self-editing skills by asking if each sentence begins with a capital and ends with a period, question mark, or exclamation point.

Sentence Formation

Verbs, nouns, adverbs, and adjectives all play significant roles in the writing process. However, for primary students, these concepts are fairly complex to understand. One instruction approach that may prove effective is to categorize a number of simple verbs, nouns, adverbs, and adjectives on index cards by color coordination. Educators can then ask one child to choose a noun card and another student to choose a verb card. The children can then face the class and read their words starting with the noun and then the verb. The students can even try reading the verb first followed by the noun. A class discussion can follow, analyzing whether or not the sentences made sense and what words might need to be added to give the sentence more meaning.

Systematic Phonics Instruction

Basic Phonic Elements

Phonics incorporates the alphabetic principle and decoding strategies. Phonics knowledge includes recognizing letter-sound correspondence. Students use phonics to sound out letter sequences and blend the sounds of the letter sequences together in order to form words.

Phonics instruction should begin with the decoding of simple syllable patterns, such as *am* and *map*. Upon mastery of simple patterns, more complex patterns can be introduced, such as *tape* or *spot*. The following characteristics are present in an effective phonics program:

1. The goal and purpose are clarified at the beginning of each lesson.

2. Visual and concrete material, such as letter cards and dry-erase boards, are used.

3. Direct instruction of letter sounds is provided through a series of mini lessons.

4. Direct instruction in the decoding of letter sounds found in words is provided, such as sounding out letters and blending sounds into words.

5. Students partake in guided and independent practice during which immediate feedback is provided. Activities such as word reading and word sorts, which incorporate previously taught spelling patterns, can reinforce explicit phonics instruction.

6. Effective phonics programs allow students to apply new phonics skills in a broad range of reading and writing contexts.

Proper Sequencing of Complex Linguistic Units

Research has shown that phonics and sight-word instruction is best accomplished using the following steps:

1. Phonics instruction should begin with **consonant sounds**. Consonant sounds block the flow of air through the mouth. Consonants can form either continuous or stop sounds. **Continuous sounds** are those that can be said for a long period of time, such as /mmm/. **Stop sounds** are said in short bursts, such as /t/.

2. The following common and regular letter combinations can be taught:

> a. **Consonant digraphs:** Consonant digraphs are combinations of two or three consonants that work together to make a single sound. Examples of consonant digraphs are *sh, ch*, and *th*.

> b. **Consonant blends:** Consonant blends are sometimes referred to as **consonant clusters**. Consonant blends occur when two or three consonant sounds are blended together to make a single consonant sound. Unlike consonant digraphs, each letter in a consonant blend is identifiable. Examples of consonant blends are *gl, gr, pl, sm*, and *sp*.

> c. **Vowel digraphs:** Vowel digraphs are sets of two vowels that spell a single sound. A diagraph is not a sound. Examples of vowel digraph pairs are *ow, ie, ae, ou, ei, ie*, and *oo*.

> d. **Diphthongs:** Diphthongs are the sounds created by letter/vowel combinations.

> e. **R- and I- controlled vowels:** These are words in which a vowel sound is controlled in a word that contains an *r, l,* or *ll* at its beginning or end. Examples include *car, girl, old,* or *call*.

3. Common inflected morphological units can be taught. **Morphological units** include word parts such as affixes or root words. Examples of morphological units that could be presented at this time are suffixes such as *-ed, -er, -est, -ing*, and *-s*.

4. Common word patterns of increasing difficulty are presented. **Word patterns** are made of sequences (or patterns) of vowels (V) and consonants (C). Examples include VC (*ear, egg, eat,* etc.), CVC (*cat, bat, map*, etc.), CCVC (*stop, frog, spot*, etc.), CVVC (*head, lead, dead*, etc.), CVCe (*same, make, rale*, etc.), etc.

5. In this stage, students are taught identification of vowel-consonant patterns and multisyllabic-word syllabication.

6. After syllabication of multisyllabic words, a discussion of why some words are irregular should occur. **Irregular words** are words that are not decodable. Students may struggle decoding some

words because the sounds of the letters found within the words do not follow predictable phonics patterns.

7. Time should be allotted for the instruction of common irregular sight words that are not readily decodable. However, this is usually not done until students are able to decode words that follow predictable phonic patterns at a rate of one letter-sound per second. Irregular sight words need to be gradually introduced. Words that are visually similar should not be shown in proximity to one another. The irregular words need to be practiced until students can read them with automaticity. New words are not introduced until the previous sets are mastered. The words are continuously reintroduced and reviewed thereafter.

8. When students first begin reading, they may be able to decode some words that have not yet been introduced to them merely by using letter-sound correspondences. The instruction of irregular words should be applied to these words as well.

Blending Consonant and Vowel Sounds to Decode Single-Syllable Words

The ability to break apart a word into its individual phonemes is referred to as **segmenting.** Segmenting words can greatly aid in a child's ability to recognize, read, and spell an entire word. In literacy instruction, **blending** is when the reader connects segmented parts to create an entire word. Segmenting and blending practice work together like pieces of a puzzle to help children practice newly-acquired vocabulary. Educators can approach segmenting and blending using a multi-sensory approach. For example, a child can manipulate letter blocks to build words and pull them apart. An educator may even ask the child to listen to the word being said and ask him or her to find the letter blocks that build each phoneme, one at a time:

/m/ /u/ /g/

/b/ /a/ /t/

/r/ /u/ /n/

Once children are able to blend and segment phonemes, they are ready for the more complex skill of blending and segmenting syllables, onsets, and rimes. Using the same multi-sensory approach, children may practice blending the syllables of familiar words on a word wall, using letter blocks, paper and pencil, or sounding them out loud. Once they blend the words together, students can then practice segmenting those same words, studying their individual syllables and the letters and sounds that create the words. Educators may again read a word out loud and ask children to write or build the first syllable, followed by the next, and so on. The very same practice can be used to identify the onset. Children can work on writing and/or building this sound followed by the word's rime. Word families and rhyming words are ideal for this type of exercise so that children can more readily see the parts of each word. Using words that rhyme can turn this exercise into a fun and engaging activity.

Once children have demonstrated the ability to independently blend and segment phonemes, syllables, onsets, and rimes, educators may present a more challenging exercise that involves **substitutions** and **deletions**. As these are more complex skills, children will likely benefit from repeated practice and modeling. Using word families and words that rhyme when teaching this skill will make the activity more enjoyable, and it will also greatly aid in a child's overall comprehension.

Substitution and Deletion Using Onset and Rime

Word	Onset Deletion	Rime Deletion	Onset Substitution	Rime Substitution
Run	un	r	Fun	rat
Bun	un	b	Gun	bat
Sun	un	s	Nun	sat

Substitution and Deletion Using Phonemes

Word	Phoneme Substitution	Phoneme Deletion
Sit	sat	si
Bit	bat	bi
Hit	hat	hi

Substitution and Deletion Using Syllables

Word	Syllable Substitution	Syllable Deletion
cement	lament or, cedar	ce
moment	statement, or motive	mo
basement	movement, or baseball	base

Consonant-Vowel Patterns

While reading has much to do with conceptual knowledge of English and awareness of the structures and rules of the language, recognizing word patterns can also help students see basic English principles. Being able to recognize familiar word patterns essentially helps students decode the pronunciation and even the meaning of unfamiliar words by recognizing core linguistic components.

The first step in identifying patterns is knowing how to sort words. When describing and searching for word patterns, sound is key. To begin, instructors can have students (or themselves) list single-syllable words that share similar beginnings, endings, and vowel sounds. Examining **affixes** (the letters before or after the root word), which change a word's initial meaning, is also key. For example, students can recognize that the *a* used in *bat* and *cat* sound the same. Recognizing this sorting method provides insight on how to pronounce the words *that* or *fat*. Thus, students gain a tool for decoding words they haven't seen before.

Teachers should also examine words that are spelled differently but sound the same. For example, *veer*, *near*, and *tier* share a sound pattern but are spelled differently. This sheds light on how the vowels *ee*, *ea*, and *ie* sound between consonants. For an activity, students can group vowel combinations into columns that indicate a shared sound to help them recognize the connection between sound and spelling patterns. Another engaging activity would be to have students create small poems that use words with a specific sound. For example, using the vowel *i*, students can be encouraged to create a rhyme with three words, each with one syllable. The results should share common vowel and consonant sounds, such as *tip*, *ship*, and *dip* or *fig*, *lip*, and *skid*. Note how the vowel remains constant even while the consonants change.

Some single-syllable words, such as common sight words, have no clear pattern. The best way to teach these words (*the*, *to*, and others) is to have students visualize and learn them just as they are. One easy activity would be to play bingo or a similar visual game using single-syllable sight words to build familiarity with the everyday terms.

Decoding Multisyllabic Words

The methodology of grouping and recognizing patterns in single-syllable words can also apply to multisyllable words. However, because these words are more complex, the pattern scope must be broader. Again, teachers must reexamine similar-sounding vowel groups and consonant relationships as with singular-syllable words. It may also help to review the six patterns of syllable spelling format: open, closed, vowel team, silent vowel *e*, consonant *le*, and *r*-controlled patterns.

As a class activity, students can spend time grouping individual words into the spelling formats to demonstrate their knowledge of English sounds and how the letters function in the words. Once explaining the categories, the instructor can even name a word and have the students say it back and then group the word into an appropriate category. For example, the word *throat* has a kind of *oh* sound because of the vowel team *oa*. Instructors should also distinguish closed- and open-syllable spelling patterns. **Open** reflects a long vowel ending sound, such as *tiger,* with an exaggerated *-er* sounding ending; alternately, the **closed** pattern reflects a short vowel sound toward the end as seen in the word *darken*.

The *r*-controlled vowels are also important to highlight. Words such as *fur* and *car* stand out because of how the *r* sounds more prevalent than the vowel. To practice this, students can list words such as *cart*, *short, turtle,* and *fertile* on the board so they can have a visual reference, or the teacher can go around the class and have students name such words aloud. Again, it's important to hear the words and examine them visually in order for students to grasp how the words function and operate.

With multisyllable words, it's important to review consonant diagraphs and how they function. Because there are many diagraphs with different pronunciations, it's important to demonstrate how they differ in various words, such as the *ch* in *Christmas* and *charity*. Students should also be able to compare how moving diagraphs within words alters pronunciations, such as with *anchor* or *pitch,* respectively.

When it comes to approaching multisyllable words in general, teachers should emphasize sounding out the words in order to grasp the pronunciation. Another good strategy for learning larger words is to have students break a word down by syllables and then combine them to complete the whole word. Again, an interactive approach to these principles will help students grasp the material more easily.

Word-Analysis Skills and Vocabulary Development

Interaction of Phonics, Syntax, and Semantics

Vocabulary

Vocabulary consists of the bank of words that children can understand and apply fluently in order to communicate effectively. A strong vocabulary and word recognition base enables children to access prior knowledge and experiences in order to make connections in written texts. A strong vocabulary also allows children to express ideas, learn new concepts, and decode the meanings of unfamiliar words by using context clues. Conversely, if a child's vocabulary knowledge is limited and does not steadily increase, reading comprehension will be negatively affected. If children become frustrated with their lack of understanding of written texts, they will likely choose to only read texts at their comfort level or refuse to read altogether. With direct instruction, educators introduce specific words to pre-teach before reading, or examine word roots, prefixes, and suffixes. Through indirect instruction, educators ensure that students are regularly exposed to new words. This engages students in high-quality conversations and social interactions and provides access to a wide variety of challenging and enjoyable reading material.

Morphology

The study of **morphology** generally deals with the structure and formation of words. A **phoneme** is the smallest unit of sound that does not necessarily carry meaning. Essentially, phonemes are combined to form words, and words are combined to form sentences. Morphology looks at the smallest meaningful part of a word, known as a **morpheme**. In contrast to a phoneme, a morpheme must carry a sound and a meaning. Free morphemes are those that can stand alone, carrying both sound and meaning, as in the following words: *girl, boy, man*, and *lady*. Just as the name suggests, **bound morphemes** are bound to other morphemes in order to carry meaning. Examples of bound morphemes include: *ish, ness, ly*, and *dis*.

Semantics

Semantics is the branch of linguistics that addresses meanings. Morphemes, words, phrases, and sentences all carry distinct meanings. The way these individual parts are arranged can have a significant effect on meaning. In order to construct language, children must be able to use semantics to arrange and rearrange words to achieve the particular meaning they are striving for. Activities that teach semantics revolve around teaching the arrangement of word parts (morphology) and root words, and then the teaching of vocabulary. Moving from vocabulary words into studying sentences and sentence structure leads children to learn how to use context clues to determine meaning and to understand anomalies such as metaphors, idioms, and allusions.

There are five types of semantic relationships that are critical to understand:

- **Hyponyms** refer to a relationship between words where general words have multiple more-specific words (hyponyms) that fall into the same category (e.g., horse: mare, stallion, foal, Appaloosa, Clydesdale).

- **Meronyms** refer to a relationship between words where a whole word has multiple parts (meronyms) that comprise it (e.g., horse: tail, mane, hooves, ears).

- **Synonyms** refer to words that have the same meaning as another word (e.g., instructor/teacher/educator, canine/dog, feline/cat, herbivore/vegetarian).

- Antonyms refer to words that have the opposite meaning as another word (e.g., true/false, up/down, in/out, right/wrong).

- **Homonyms** refer to words that are spelled the same (homographs) or sound the same (**homophones**) but mean different things (e.g., there/their/they're, two/too/to, principal/principle, plain/plane, (kitchen) sink/ sink (down as in water)).

Syntax

With its origins from the Greek word, "syntaxis," which means arrangement, **syntax** is the study of phrase and sentence formation. The study of syntax focuses on the ways in which specific words can be combined to create coherent meaning. For example: the simple rearrangement of the words, "I can run," is different from the question, "Can I run?" which is also different from the meaningless "Run I can."

The following methods can be used to teach syntax:

- Proper Syntax Modeling: Students don't need to be corrected for improper syntax. Instead, they should be shown ways to rephrase what they said with proper syntax. If a student says, "Run I can," then the teacher should say, "Oh, you can run how fast?" This puts syntax in place with conversational skills.

- Open-Ended Sentences: Students can complete open-ended sentences with proper syntax both orally and in written format, or they can correct sentences that have improper syntax so that they make sense.

- Listening for Syntax: Syntax is auditory. Students can often hear a syntax error before they can see it in writing. Teachers should have students use word cards or word magnets to arrange and rearrange simple sentences and read them aloud to check for syntax.

- Repetition: Syntax can be practiced by using songs, poems, and rhymes for repetitive automation.

Pragmatics

Pragmatics is the study of what words mean in certain situations. It helps to understand the intentions and interpretations of intentions through words used in human interaction. Different listeners and different situations call for different language and intonations of language. When people engage in a conversation, it is usually to convey a certain message, and the message (even using the same words) can change depending on the setting and the audience. The more fluent the speaker, the more success she or he will have in conveying the intended message.

The following methods can be used to teach pragmatics:

- When students state something incorrectly, a response can be given to what they intended to say in the first place. For instance, if a student says, "That's how it didn't happen." Then the teacher might say, "Of course, that's not how it happened." Instead of putting students on defense by being corrected, this method puts them at ease and helps them learn.

- Role-playing conversations with different people in different situations can help teach pragmatics. For example, pretend playing can be used where a situation remains the same but the audience changes, or the audience stays the same but the situations change. This can be followed with a discussion about how language and intonations change too.

- Different ways to convey a message can be used, such as asking vs. persuading, or giving direct vs. indirect requests and polite vs. impolite messages.

- Various non-verbal signals can be used to see how they change pragmatics. For example, students can be encouraged to use mismatched words and facial expressions, such as angry words while smiling or happy words while pretending to cry.

Strategies to Help Read New and/or Difficult Words

Children who are developing reading fluency and comprehension skills can become frustrated when presented with unfamiliar words in a given text. With direct phonics instruction, educators can teach children to decode words and then use context clues to define the words while reading. If children have a strong enough understanding of language structures, including nouns and verbs, educators can ask them to consider what part of speech the unknown word might be based on and where it might fit into the sentence. Other useful strategies involve **self-monitoring**, in which children are asked to think as they read and ask themselves if what they have just read makes sense. Focusing on visual clues, such as drawings and photographs, may give children valuable insight into deciphering unknown words. Looking for the word in another section of the text to see how it relates to the overall meaning could give a clue to the new vocabulary word. Spelling the word out loud or looking for word chunks, prefixes, and suffixes, as well as demonstrating how to segment the unknown word into its individual syllables, may also be effective strategies to employ.

One of the most valuable strategies, however, for helping children to read and understand new words is **pre-teaching**. In this strategy, educators select what they evaluate to be the unfamiliar words in the text and then introduce them to the class before reading. Educators using this method should be careful not to simply ask the children to read the text and then spell the new words correctly. They should also provide clear definitions and give the children the opportunity to read these words in various sentences to decipher word meaning. This method can dramatically reduce how often children stop reading in order to reflect on unknown words. Educators are often unsure as to whether to correct every mispronounced word a child makes when reading. If the mispronounced word still makes sense, it is sometimes better to allow the child to continue to read, since the more the child stops, the more the child's reading comprehension and fluency are negatively affected.

Applying Word Analysis Skills

Phonics and decoding skills aid the analysis of new words. **Word analysis** is the ability to recognize the relationships between the spelling, syllabication, and pronunciation of new and/or unfamiliar words. Having a clear understanding of word structure, orthography, and the meaning of morphemes also aid in the analysis of new words.

However, not all words follow predictable phonics patterns, morphology, or orthography. Such irregular words must be committed to memory and are called sight words.

Phonics skills, syllabic skills, structural analysis, word analysis, and memorization of sight words lead to word recognition automaticity. **Word recognition** is the ability to correctly and automatically recognize words in or out of context. Word recognition is a prerequisite for fluent reading and reading comprehension.

Reading Unfamiliar Multisyllabic Words

Reading competence of multisyllabic words is accomplished through phonics skills that are accompanied with a reader's ability to recognize morphological structures within words. **Structural analysis** is a word recognition skill that focuses on the meaning of word parts, or morphemes, during the introduction of a new word. Therefore, the instruction of structural analysis focuses on the recognition and application of morphemes. **Morphemes** are word parts such as base words, prefixes, inflections, and suffixes. Students can use structural analysis skills to find familiar word parts within an unfamiliar word in order to decode the word and determine the definition of the new word. Identification and association of such word segments also aids the proper pronunciation and spelling of new multisyllabic words.

Similarly, learning to apply phonics skills to longer and more complex words relies on a reader's ability to recognize syllable structures within multisyllabic words. **Syllabic analysis**, or **syllabication**, is a word analysis skill that helps students split words into syllables. **Syllables** are phonological units that contain a vowel sound. Students may be intimidated by long, multisyllabic words. Helping students break up multisyllabic words into morphological units (structural analysis) and phonological units according to syllable types makes longer words appear as a connected series of smaller words. The identified syllables can then be blended, pronounced, and/or written together as a single word. This helps students learn to decode and encode the longer words more accurately and efficiently with less anxiety. Thus, syllabic analysis leads to the rapid word recognition that is critical in reading fluency and comprehension.

The following table identifies the six basic syllable patterns that should be explicitly taught during syllabic instruction:

Basic Syllable Patterns		
Name of Syllable Type	Characteristics of Syllable Type	Examples
Closed	A syllable with a single vowel closed in by a consonant.	lab, bog, an
Open	A syllable that ends with a single vowel. Note that the letter *y* acts as a vowel.	go, me, sly
Vowel-Consonant-Silent *e*	A syllable with a single vowel followed by a consonant then *e*.	like, rake, note, obese
Vowel Teams	A syllable that has two consecutive vowels. Note that the letters *w* and *y* act as vowels.	meat, pertain, bay, toad, window
R-controlled	A syllable with one or two vowels followed by the letter *r*.	car, jar, fir, sir, collar, turmoil
Consonant *le (-al, -el)* Also called final stable	A syllable that has a consonant followed by the letters *le*, *al*, or *el*.	puddle, stable, uncle, bridal, pedal
Other final stable syllables	A syllable at the end of words can be taught as a recognizable unit such as *cious, age, ture, tion*, or *sion*.	pension, elation, puncture, stumpage, fictitious

Using Context

Reference materials are the most obvious way students can independently learn the definition and pronunciation of new vocabulary terms.

When using **contextual strategies**, students are introduced to new words indirectly within a sentence or paragraph. Contextual strategies require students to infer the meaning of a word by utilizing semantic and contextual clues.

The use of appositives and parenthetical elements can be very effective contextual strategies. **Appositives** are words or a group of words that add meaning or define a term that directly precedes them. An example of a sentence that includes apposition is: "Strawberries, heart-shaped and red berries, are delicious when eaten right off of the vine." In this sentence, the definition of strawberries ("heart shaped and red berries") directly follows the term and is introduced with and closes with a comma. **Parenthetical elements** are specific types of appositives that add details to a term but not necessarily a definition. For example: "My cat, the sweetest in the whole world, didn't come home last night." In this sentence, the parenthetical element ("the sweetest in the whole world") further describes the cat but does not provide a definition of the word "cat."

Structural analysis skills are beneficial in the pronunciation of new words. When readers use **structural analysis**, they recognize affixes or roots as meaningful word parts within a word. When a new word doesn't contain parts that are recognized by a student, the reader can use phonic letter–sound patterns to divide the word into syllables. The word parts can then be combined to yield the proper pronunciation.

Word maps are visual organizers that promote structural analysis skills for vocabulary development. **Word maps** may require students to define or provide synonyms, antonyms, and pictures for given vocabulary terms. Alternatively, **morphological maps** may be used to relate words that share a common morpheme.

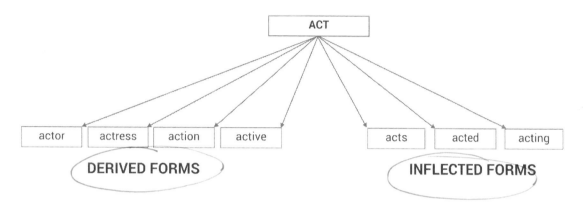

Similarly, **word webs** are used to compare and classify a list of words. Word webs show relationships between new words and a student's background knowledge. With the main concept placed centrally within the word web, secondary and tertiary terms stem off from this central concept.

The table below identifies additional ways in which teachers can help students independently define unfamiliar words or words with multiple meanings:

Strategy	Examples
By Definition: Look up the word in a dictionary or thesaurus. Helps students realize that a single word can have multiple meanings.	Her favorite fruit to eat was a date. He went on a date with his girlfriend.
By Example: Invite students to offer their own examples, or to state their understanding following your own examples.	A myth is a story attempting to explain a natural phenomenon, such as the story of Prometheus to understand fire.
By Synonym: Understand that words have many different meanings. Some words are better synonyms than others.	She was very happy that day; her face was *radiant* with joy.
By Antonym: Teach student to look for words that have opposite meanings if the context of the sentence calls for its opposite.	Hannah was not happy that day; she was, in fact, very *depressed*.
By Apposition: **Apposition** is when the definition is given within the sentence.	The mango, a round, yellow, juicy fruit with an enormous seed in the middle, was ripe enough to eat.
By Origin: Identify Greek and Latin roots to figure out meanings of words.	In the word *hypertension*, the root "*hyper*" is a Greek word meaning "above" or "over."
By Context: Identifying what a word means by the surrounding text.	Water evaporates when it becomes hot, and the liquid turns into gas.

Developing Word Consciousness and Vocabulary Knowledge

Word consciousness can be developed through structural analysis of word parts and words origins. Identification of word segments will enable students to more readily master new words.

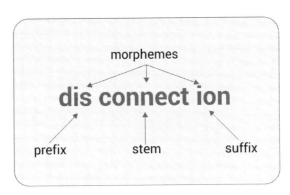

Students can develop a love of words through word games, which create a safe environment to take linguistic risks and feel successful. Examples include sight word games, word memory games, or games that require students to create new words using an assigned list of affixes and roots.

A **word sort** is an example of a word game that can be used to develop word consciousness. Using a set of word cards prepared by the teacher, students decide how to separate the cards into categories. Students are then asked to explain why they grouped a set of words together.

Students also learn to love words by sharing new and interesting words they encounter through independent reading or when they are taught new words explicitly by the teacher. Students can share new words on an online word blog or word cloud, a word wall within the classroom, or a word list contained within a notebook. These tools help to personalize vocabulary instruction while improving students' flexibility and fluency.

Schema development for easier word acquisition can be developed by dividing these word lists into categories based on similarities or differences. The list of new words should be referred to often in order to increase the students' exposure. To further strengthen comprehension, students should be required to utilize the words in writing and discussion activities.

Vocabulary Knowledge
Vocabulary knowledge is an indicator and predictor of comprehension. If students find a match between a word within a text and a word that they've learned through listening and speaking, they are likelier to recognize and understand the meaning of the word in the written context. As the students will spend less time decoding and interpreting the word, they are likelier to read fluently and with comprehension. In contrast, if students cannot connect a written word to a word within their speaking or listening vocabulary, their fluency and comprehension may be interrupted. This proves to be true even if the student is able to correctly pronounce the word.

Word Reference Materials

Words can have different meanings depending on how they are used in a text. There are several methods for helping students decipher word meanings:

Students should be taught to effectively use a dictionary and a thesaurus, including digital dictionaries and resources. Students need to know how to read the **dictionary**, so they understand that there can be more than one meaning for a particular word. Dictionaries also help teach word pronunciation and syllables. A **thesaurus** teaches antonyms and synonyms. Once students know the correct meaning and pronunciation, they are able to better understand the context of the word in the text.

Reading Fluency and Comprehension

Automatic Word Recognition

Word recognition occurs when students are able to correctly and automatically recognize and read a word. Phonics and sight word instruction help with the promotion of accurate and automatic word identification and word recognition. Once students are able to readily identify and recognize words, their attention is not devoted toward the dissection of word interpretation, and they can focus on the meaning of the text, supporting reading comprehension skills.

Phonics instruction stresses letter-sound correspondences and the manipulation of phonemes. Through phonics instruction, students learn the relationships between the letters and symbols of written language and the sounds of spoken language. It is through the application of phonics principles that students are able to decode words. When a word is **decoded,** the letters that make up the printed word are translated into sounds. When students are able to recognize and manipulate letter-sound relationships of single-syllable words, they are able to apply such relationships to decode more complex words. In this way, phonics aids reading fluency and reading comprehension.

Sight words, sometimes referred to as **high-frequency words**, are words that are used often but may not follow the regular principles of phonics. Sight words may also be defined as words that students are able to readily recognize and read without having to sound them out. Students are encouraged to memorize words by sight so their reading fluency is not deterred through the frequent decoding of regularly- occurring irregular words. In this way, sight word recognition aids reading fluency and reading comprehension.

Reading Fluency

Several factors influence a student's reading development skills. Students learn to read at varying ages. A student's background knowledge, first language acquisition, and family involvement in reading all affect a student's progress. Therefore, when to introduce fluency instruction cannot be determined merely by a student's age or grade level. Fluency instruction begins when a student can use basic decoding skills and can read 90% of connected text with accuracy. Routinely assessing a student's decoding and accuracy skills will help to determine when to begin fluency instruction.

Even if students don't yet display automaticity, modeling can be used to initially introduce fluency. Modeling demonstrates social norms of reading rate and prosody while building vocabulary, academic language, and background knowledge.

Practice, Guidance, and Feedback
Accuracy and reading rate are fundamental components of fluency, but it's important to remember that practice is an essential component of effective fluency instruction. When teachers provide daily opportunities for students to learn words and utilize word-analysis skills, accuracy and rate are likely to increase.

Oral reading accompanied by guidance and feedback from teachers, peers, and/or parents has been shown to significantly improve fluency. In order to be beneficial, such feedback needs to provide targeted and differentiated advice on areas where a student needs improvement. It's also recommended that teachers provide feedback that includes a variety of strategies.

Research-Based, Systematic, Explicit Strategies That Improve Fluency and Accuracy
Word-reading accuracy requires that students have a strong understanding of letter-sound correspondence and the ability to accurately blend the sounds together. Providing systematic, explicit instruction in phonemic awareness, phonics, and decoding skills will cultivate such accuracy. When students are readily able to identify high-frequency sight words, their accuracy improves. Therefore, instructors should provide ample opportunities to practice these words.

Research-Based, Systematic, Explicit Strategies That Improve Fluency and Reading Rate
Reading aloud has proven effective in strengthening reading fluency. Whisper-reading accompanied by teacher monitoring has also proven effective for students who don't yet display automaticity in their decoding skills. Timed reading of sight phrases or stories also improves fluency with respect to rate. During a **timed-reading** exercise, the number of words read in a given amount of time is recorded. Routinely administering timed readings and displaying the results in graphs and charts has been shown to increase student motivation.

Timed-repeated readings, where a student reads and re-reads familiar texts in a given time, is a commonly used instructional strategy to increase reading speed, accuracy, and comprehension. Students read and re-read the passage until they reach their target rate.

Name_____

MY FLUENCY GRAPH

	week 1	week 2	week 3	week 4	week 5	week 6	week 7	week 8	week 9
150									
145									
140									
135									
130									
125									
120									
115									
110									
105									
100									
95									
90									
85									
80									
75									
70									
65									
60									
55									
50									
45									
40									
35									
30									
25									
20									
15									
10									
5									

Research-Based, Systematic, Explicit Strategies That Improve Fluency and Prosody

Reading aloud not only improves the rate but also encourages appropriate expression, or **prosody**. When the teacher, the student, or an entire student body reads aloud, students become more exposed to the use of prosody; therefore, their reading expression is strengthened. When teachers read aloud, they model prosody, which cues students to the social norms of pace, pauses, inflection, emotion, and tone when reading different types of text. In **choral reading**, all students in the class read a passage aloud together, which allows them to hear text being read accurately and with good pacing and phrasing. By having students listen to recordings of themselves reading, teachers promote independent judgment and goal setting.

Reading theaters are another effective instructional practice that supports prosody. During reading theater instruction, students are assigned a character in a play. The emphasis is reading aloud with a purpose. Students use prosody to share their interpretations and understandings of their assigned characters' personalities and roles.

Phrase-cued reading is a third strategy that aids the development of prosody. During phrase-cued reading, teachers read a text aloud and mark where they pause or show intonation, emphasis, tone, inflections, and/or expression.

How to Address a Range of Needs

Several strategies can be implemented to assist English Language Learners, speakers of nonstandard English, advanced learners, and readers who have reading difficulties or disabilities. However, it's always important to provide each student with reading materials and strategies that are appropriate for his or her specific reading level and area of concern.

Struggling readers, students with reading difficulties or disabilities, and students with special needs benefit from direct instruction and feedback that teaches decoding and analysis of unknown words, automaticity in key sight words, and correct expression and phrasing. These learners also benefit from oral support. This may be provided through scaffolded reading, choral reading, partner reading, books on tape, and computer programs. Teachers should consistently offer opportunities for students to practice repeated reading, and should gradually introduce more challenging reading levels as students progress.

English Language Learners and speakers of nonstandard English benefit from explicit instruction in vocabulary development in order to aid accuracy, rate, and reading comprehension. Providing ample opportunities to read orally with a scaffolding approach also helps this group. For instance, teachers may read a short passage and have students immediately read it back to them. Direct instruction in English intonation patterns, syntax, and punctuation are effective tools in assisting English language learners with the development of prosody.

In order to broaden and enhance fluency for advanced learners, teachers should gradually introduce more advanced texts across several content areas.

Continued Assessment of Student Fluency

Assessment of fluency must include entry-level assessments, progress monitoring, and summative assessments of accuracy, rate, and prosody. The results should be analyzed and interpreted in order to adjust instruction and provide struggling readers with proper interventions. Regular assessments also help teachers to construct differentiated instruction in order to address the fluency needs of advanced learners.

Assessing Students' Word-Reading Accuracy

Running records, a widely used fluency assessment, allows teachers to document error patterns in reading accuracy as students read benchmark books. As the student reads aloud, the teacher holds a copy of the same text and records any omissions, mispronunciations, and substitutions. With this information, teachers can determine which fluency strategies a student does or doesn't employ.

Using Timed Contextual Oral Reading to Assess Fluency and Rate

Assessment of reading rate often begins with sight-word reading automaticity. Automaticity assessment may also include the decoding of non-words in order to determine if a student is able to decode words using sound-syllable correspondence.

Among the most commonly used measurements of reading rate is oral contextual timed reading. During a **timed reading**, the number of errors made within a given amount of time is recorded. This data can be used to identify if a student's rate is improving and if reading rate falls within the recommended fluency rates for the student's grade level. If a student's reading rate is below average, any of the previously identified research-based, systematic, explicit strategies that improve fluency with respect to rate may be applied.

One common timed assessment for reading accuracy is the **WCPM**, the words-correct-per-minute assessment. The teacher presents an unfamiliar text to a student and asks the student to read aloud for one minute. As the student reads, the teacher records any omissions, mispronunciations, or substitutions. These errors are subtracted by the total number of words in the text to determine a score, which is then compared to oral reading fluency norms. With this assessment, teachers can select the appropriate level of text for each student.

Recommended Reading Fluency Rates		
Grade	**Semester**	**Correct Words Per Minute**
First Grade	Winter	38
	Spring	40 – 60
Second Grade	Fall	55
	Winter	73 – 79
	Spring	81 – 93
Third Grade	Fall	79
	Winter	83 – 92
	Spring	100 – 115
Fourth Grade	Fall	91 – 99
	Winter	98 – 113
	Spring	106 – 119
Fifth Grade	Fall	105
	Winter	109 – 118
	Spring	118 – 128

Assessing Prosody Through Observation of Connected-Text Reading
In order to assess prosody, a teacher listens for inflection, expression, and pauses as the student reads a connected text aloud. The Integrate Reading Performance Record Oral Reading Fluency Scale designed by the National Assessment of Educational Progress (NAEP) is also used to assess prosody. Students at levels 3 and 4 are considered to be fluent with respect to prosody. Students at levels 1 and 2 are considered to be non-fluent in prosody.

- Level 4: Reads mainly in large phrase groups. The structure of the story is intact and the author's syntax is consistent, even if there are some deviations from the text. Most of the story is read with expression.

- Level 3: Reads mainly in three- or four-word phrase groups. Majority of phrasing is appropriate and preserves syntax of the author. Little expression is present with interpreting the text.

- Level 2: Reads two-word phrases with some three- or four-word groupings. Word-by-word reading may occur. Some word groupings may seem awkward and indicates the larger context is not being paid attention to.

- Level 1: Reads word-by-word. Some occasional two-or-three word phrases may be present, but they are not frequent or they don't preserve meaningful syntax.

Linguistic, Sociological, Cultural, Cognitive, and Psychological Reading Processes

Much of a student's reading comprehension will be influenced by their individual perspective and upbringing. Cultural and social values inform the way children think from a young age, and these factors play a major role in their cognition and psychological development. Therefore, it's important to understand that some students, including those learning English as a second language, may not interpret reading the way a typical native English speaker would. The role of the teacher is to be respectful and receptive of students' understanding of reading and guide them in drawing correct analysis. Being mindful of cultural differences will enable instructors to understand how their students think, or at least help identify any disconnects, to tailor instruction appropriately.

Different cultures may not share some of the values, goals, or general views Americans share. For example, Americans tend to be skeptical of and question leadership, yet another culture might put trust more easily in leadership and find questioning authority to be counterproductive or seditious. This alternate view of the subject matter may result in difficulty understanding the concepts when reading a passage on such a topic. It's important to remember that, although outside and individual views are not wrong, students should be able to draw an accurate analysis of reading content. Reading confusion can be avoided through simple, yet thorough, linguistic training.

Instructors should strive to focus on basic rules of English. Students must know how English works and sounds before they can connect meaning to sentences. Again, each student learns differently, so individualized instruction might be needed to help students who are having issues with the material. This approach is also known as **scaffolding**.

The **input hypothesis of language learning** suggests that students can make breakthroughs in language comprehension when they are exposed to material slightly above their current level. It's important not to overwhelm students but to be patient with them through complex material; the result will be that they can read and understand a variety of other texts after mastering difficult reading concepts. However, if the material is too difficult, easier reading may be substituted.

Differentiating Literal, Inferential, and Evaluative Comprehension

Literal Reading Comprehension
The first level of reading comprehension is **literal meaning**. The word "literal" refers to an author's exact message or meaning. What is the author directly telling the reader? Literal comprehension is the direct meaning of the text, which may include setting, main idea, sequencing, elements of story, and cause/effect. Once word analysis is mastered, readers can begin to master literal reading comprehension. When a reader can **decode,** he or she can fluently read a text and understand its meaning. Readers use **text evidence** (facts, hints, and statistics, provided by the author to help support ideas or theories within texts) to further understand texts. When students identify text evidence, instructors are able to evaluate and assess whether students comprehend the questions being asked, and determine the students' ability to locate answers within a story. Citing evidence is extremely helpful during whole group discussions. Students can note the page, exact line, and paragraph where the answer was found. This literal understanding and response to questions helps struggling readers follow along, while aiding them in the learning process.

Inferential Reading Comprehension
The second level of reading comprehension is interpreting and forming the **inferential meaning of texts**. Inferential reading comprehension refers to "reading between the lines." "Reading between the lines" forces the reader to make generalizations from the text using text evidence. It is necessary for readers

to have a complete understanding of the text in order to make inferences. A reader needs to understand the direct message, and then interpret the indirect meaning behind it. Responses to questions may not be directly stated in the text; however, the answer must be figuratively inferred by perceiving the implied meaning. Inferencing may involve details from the story, sequencing, themes, drawing conclusions or making generalizations, and cause and effect relationships. As a reader's comprehension skills improve, his or her ability to form inferences also strengthens. Word analysis and direct literal comprehension must be mastered prior to young readers forming inferences; students may struggle to make inferences without prior mastery of these two skills.

Evaluating Reading Comprehension

The third level of reading comprehension is the ability to **evaluate the text**. Evaluating reading comprehension builds upon literal and inferential comprehension. Readers must be able to take the entire text and evaluate it for various criteria. A fluent reader may be able to recognize an author's bias once he or she forms and understands inferences. **Bias** is a personal opinion revealed throughout a text, based on comments or word choices. A reader must be able to evaluate unsupported assumptions, propaganda, and faulty reasoning in the text. Propaganda is meant to help or harm a particular group. An author's personal feeling(s) or bias may be decoded through small details and subtleties throughout the text. A reader should assess assumptions made by the author, and distinguish between fact and opinion. An author's opinions can lead to faulty reasoning. It is the reader's job to distinguish and separate the facts from the author's biases. Readers may also be asked to use evidence from the text to support their reaction to the text or towards characters. Evaluating themes is a difficult task and utilizes a reader's inferential understanding of a text to evaluate the overall purpose of the text. Use of language and the role of text structure and syntax play an important role in a reader's understanding of a text. The complexity of a text may impede a reader's understanding.

Comprehension Strategies

A teacher "think-aloud" is a great strategy to promote the development of comprehension skills and eventually transfer these skills to written language. Students who are allowed to stop periodically throughout the text to verbalize what they have read score significantly higher on standardized testing. Teacher read-alouds help promote listening comprehension skills because students can listen without having to decode the text. Students can freely take notes and outline what they hear, and can listen for reading strategies, such as word and voice emphasis. In small intervention groups, a teacher can read aloud shorter texts to help teach reading comprehension. Rather than having students read aloud during smaller group work, teachers can help promote comprehension by simply having students listen to books catered to their reading level, and then having think-alouds in small groups. Students can complete graphic organizers or comprehension worksheets during listening comprehension time.

Independent Reading

Independent reading strategies promote healthy reading for pleasure and enjoyment. Hopefully, these strategies promote a lifelong love of reading. Students should be given daily, independent reading time in the classroom. Teachers phrase this time as **D.E.A.R.** or "Drop Everything and Read" time. Typically, this time can be incorporated into a teacher's reading block. It is suggested that students have about 20 minutes of D.E.A.R. time daily. Students can read a book from home, the library, or one selected from the variety of books found within the classroom.

Teachers are required to have a classroom library. Some schools require a certain number of books or filled bookcases within a classroom. The library center should also contain more than just books. The classroom library should be an inviting environment for students. Small lamps make the area warmer—like home rather than school—and provide extra light for reading. Furniture—such as beanbag chairs, pillows, and small chairs—allow students to get comfortable, rather than reading at their desk. Not only is the environment important, but the reading center must also be an organized, designated space. If books are disorganized in the classroom library, students may be deterred from using the space appropriately, simply because they cannot find what they are looking for, or out of shear frustration. Organizing books by theme or genre helps students search for the books they desire. For students in younger grades, books should be grouped in plastic tubs using picture and word category labels like "animals" or "holidays." This organization method is especially helpful to those learning to read.

A listening center is also another helpful space in the classroom library. In the listening center, students listen to stories that are played through a sound device (like a CD or MP3 player) and follow along in the text. A teacher can switch the book out weekly to match a theme in the classroom, or can leave a "free choice bin" for students to choose what they would like to listen to. Again, listening to the story will encourage and emphasize reading strategies, such as voice and pacing.

Having a bookshelf with the teacher's or students' text selections may encourage readers to select a good book quickly. Some students enjoy re-reading a book from a teacher read aloud; therefore, placing it in the "teacher's pick" area may encourage developing readers to pick it up. Students also like to follow their classmates. Therefore, teachers should have a section where students can place a book that students can recommend to their friends. For older students, brief recommendation sheets can be filled out by the students. These sheets briefly list a few of a book's main themes so that potential readers can see if they are interested in reading the book. Reading from basal readers and school texts do not necessarily encourage reading for pleasure, as they are texts that are chosen by the school and instructor. For this reason, silent reading time is so important. Silent reading time gives students options and a chance to make their own choices. Students can choose the book and the appropriate reading pace when reading independently.

Independent Reading and Family and Community Involvement

The following are strategies for promoting purposeful and independent reading of a wide variety of texts:

- Promote independent reading of narrative, literary, expository, and informational texts.
- Teach students how to select books that are at appropriate reading levels.
- Use students' personal interests to help motivate them to read independently.
- Provide structured reading opportunities in class.
- Encourage independent reading at home.
- Monitor students' independent reading.

In addition to teacher read-alouds, as discussed earlier, students should have approximately twenty minutes per day to read independently. This time should be structured and occur at predictable times each day or throughout the week. Students should be encouraged to read a variety of texts at this time (narrative, literary, expository, and informational texts). Students also should read independently.

In order to benefit from independent reading, students must read texts that are appropriate for their assessed reading level. Therefore, students should be aware of their reading levels and be able to select texts that coincide with this level. For students in primary school, the **five-finger test** can be used in the text-selection process. The five-finger test asserts that if a student has trouble with five or more words on a randomly selected page, then the book is above that student's reading level. For older readers, the teacher can group texts into levels and/or categories, from which students can select based on their personal interests.

In order for independent reading time to be effective, students should be accountable for what is read. A great assessment tool is to have each student give an oral report of one book that they have read during the marking period. Students should be given nightly reading homework as well. Teachers may require students to log the number of minutes read each night. Such reading logs should require parents to sign next to the number of minutes a night a child has read.

Reading Comprehension Strategies for Fiction and Poetry

Independent and Reflective Reading

Introducing students to a variety of literature and writing styles is very important for their development. For one thing, different types of literature will present different content, themes, and linguistic structures that utilize critical-thinking and analysis skills. Students should be able to distinguish the themes and motivations of the author and draw meaning from the words themselves.

In addition to developing basic reading comprehension skills, a broad literary selection will help students enjoy reading. Enjoyment and engagement are key motivators in the learning process. If students have fun reading short stories or excerpts from novels, they will want to continue reading. Thus, their hunger for more reading will grow, and so will their skill set as they delve into more advanced literature. Mixing popular texts and more classical stories will give students a wide range of styles and varying perspectives.

Each fiction genre tends to have shared themes or common tropes. If an instructor chooses, he or she can structure reading selections to explore several excerpts from individual genres and have students reflect on their similarities and differences within each genre. In all reading selections, instructors should encourage students to decipher meaning within the text and strive for them to draw their own analysis of the writing. Therefore, selections must be challenging enough to encourage debate but with language that isn't too complex so that new readers can grasp the content clearly.

Poetry should be used in class; it is yet another source of literary enjoyment. Poetry also offers another way for students to analyze meaning and language. For beginning readers, narrative-focused poetry may be ideal to use in lessons. *Paul Revere's Ride* by Henry Wadsworth Longfellow is an example of a poem that offers easy-to-follow language, rhyme, and a narrative that bears historical significance. This is an excellent poem to introduce new readers to American poetry. In poems, students should analyze where rhymes are present and discuss the word choice the poet uses. Instructors should also introduce the elements of poetry, such as meter, stanzas, and other literary devices. Naturally, more advanced poems can also be studied based on how strong the students' reading skills are.

Comprehending Fiction

Some important story elements in teaching reading comprehension include character, plot, problem/solution, and setting. Some inferential aspects of reading comprehension are mood, tone, theme, point of view, and voice. These elements are more difficult to teach and for students to master. Repetition and understanding improves mastery of these inferential aspects, particularly when they are broken into independent lessons.

Literary Genres

Genre is a method of categorizing literature by form, content, style, and technique. When selections of literature share enough characteristics and literary elements, they are classified into the same genre. Genre is more than just a categorization system, though; genre identifies literature by its communicative purpose. Authors write to accomplish any of a variety of social purposes: to inform, to explain, to entertain, to persuade, to maintain relationships, and so on. All types of texts fall into one of the following five genres: fiction, nonfiction, poetry, drama, and folklore. Each of these has a variety of subgenres. A particular piece of writing may fall into more than one genre or subgenre.

A variety of texts must be used to teach literature and reading. Folklore and poetry both have aspects to enhance comprehension. Poetry teaches lyrical reading and emphasis; it is written with specific structure and rhythm. There are many types of poetry, such as ballads, lyrics, couplets, epics, and sonnets. Poetry teaches students about adhering to punctuation while reading and allows students to read with pauses. A great teaching strategy to employ with poetry lessons is the use of blank poetry books that students can use to take notes and create their own specific poems. Poetry contains similes, personification, and onomatopoeia; therefore, poems are a great way to teach imagery and figurative language.

Drama, or plays, can emphasize voice, and gives students the option to take on a role of a character. One way to teach drama is to divide students into groups and host a reader's theater. Students and teachers have a lot of fun preparing to present a play in front of the class. Prose text covers a wide range of literature from novels, to folklore, to biographies. Developing a unit dedicated to the various types of folklore (short stories, tall tales, myth, legend, and fantasy) can be creative and fun for students. Autobiographies, biographies, and historical fiction can help teach facts. Providing students with the opportunity to research a person in history and present the findings to the class develops comprehension, presentation, speaking, writing, and research skills.

Recognizing Different Genres

Reading is fundamental to learning. Reading nurtures imagination, critical thinking, communication skills, and social competence. Many children are drawn to the allure of reading and often their attention is captivated by a certain type of book or books about a particular personal interest. It is important to introduce them to an eclectic selection of text types. Cultural knowledge, a more intricate worldview, and a host of new vocabulary can be built through the experience of diverse literature. Reading a wide range of writing styles brings students into contact with many characters and lifestyles. Reading varied texts sparks different emotions in a child and teaches a variety of means of expression. In this way, children deepen social and emotional skills. In short, reading a wide variety of texts produces a well-rounded education and prepares children for their experience of the world.

<u>Fiction</u>

Fiction is imaginative text that is invented by the author. Fiction is characterized by the following literary elements:

- **Characters:** the people, animals, aliens, or other living figures the story is about
- **Setting:** the location, surroundings, and time the story takes place in
- **Conflict:** a dilemma the characters face either internally or externally
- **Plot:** the sequence and the rise and fall of excitement in the action of a story
- **Resolution:** the solution to the conflict that is discovered as a result of the story
- **Point of View:** the lens through which the reader experiences the story
- **Theme:** the moral to the story or the message the author is sending to the reader

Historical Fiction

Historical fiction is a story that occurs in the past and uses a realistic setting and authentic time period characters. Historical fiction usually has some historically accurate events mixed and balanced with invented plot and characters.

Science Fiction

Science fiction is an invented story that occurs in the future or an alternate universe. It often deals with space, time travel, robots, or aliens, and highly-advanced technology.

Fantasy

Fantasy is a subgenre of fiction that involves magic or supernatural elements and/or takes place in an imaginary world. Examples include talking animals, superheroes rescuing the day, or characters taking on a mythical journey or quest.

Mystery and Adventure

Mystery fiction is a story that involves a puzzle or crime to be solved by the main characters. The mystery is driven by suspense and foreshadowing. The reader must sift through clues and distractions to solve the puzzle with the protagonist. **Adventure stories** are driven by the risky or exciting action that happens in the plot.

Realistic and Contemporary Fiction

Realistic fiction depends on the author portraying the world without speculation. The characters are ordinary, and the action could happen in real life. The conflict often involves growing up, family life, or learning to cope with some significant emotion or challenge.

<u>Nonfiction Literature</u>

Nonfiction literature is text that is true and accurate in detail. Nonfiction can cover virtually any topic in the natural world. Nonfiction writers conduct research and carefully organize facts before writing. Nonfiction has the following subgenres:

- **Informational Text:** This is text written to impart information to the reader. It may have literary elements such as charts, graphs, indexes, glossaries, or bibliographies.

- **Persuasive Text:** This is text that is meant to sway the reader to have a particular opinion or take a particular action.

- **Biographies and Autobiographies:** This is text that tells intimate details of someone's life. If an author writes the text about someone else, it is a **biography**. If the author writes it about himself or herself, it is an **autobiography.**

- **Communicative text:** This is text used to communicate with another person. This includes such texts as emails, formal and informal letters, and tweets. This content often consists of two-sided dialogue between people.

Drama
Drama is any writing that is intended to be performed in front of an audience, such as plays, and TV and movie scripts. Dialogue and action are central to convey the author's theme. **Comedy** is any drama designed to be funny or lighthearted. **Tragedy** is any drama designed to be serious or sad.

Poetry
This is text that is written in verse and has a rhythmic cadence. It often involves descriptive imagery, rhyming stanzas, and beautiful mastery of language. It is often personal, emotional, and introspective. Poetry is often considered a work of art.

Folklore
Folklore is literature that has been handed down from generation to generation by word of mouth. Folklore is not based in fact but in unsubstantiated beliefs. It is often very important to a culture or custom. The following are some common types of folklore:

- **Fairy Tales:** These are usually written for children and often carry a moral or universal truth. They are stories written about fairies or other magical creatures.

- **Fables:** Similar to fairy tales, fables are written for children and include tales of supernatural people or animals that speak like people. They often are built around a moral lesson.

- **Myths:** These tales are often about the gods, include symbolism, and may involve historical events and reveal human behavior. Sometimes they tell how historical things came about.

- **Legends:** Exaggerated and only partially truthful, these are tales of heroes and significant events.

- **Tall Tales:** Often funny stories and sometimes set in the Wild West, these are tales that contain extreme exaggeration and were never true.

Literary Response and Analysis Skills

Structural Elements of a Plot
There are five main structural elements of a plot:

1. **Exposition:** This is where the author introduces characters and establishes the setting.

2. **Rising Action:** This is where the conflict starts to develop and complications may form.

3. **Climax:** This is when the conflict is at its highest moment.

4. **Falling Action:** This is where characters make choices that will determine the end result.

5. **Resolution:** This is how the story ends and overall the outcome.

Characters

When readers compare and contrast characters, it is important that they ask themselves three questions:

1. Why compare/contrast characters?
2. What is compared/contrast between characters?
3. How are they the same/different?

Setting

Evaluating the relevance of the setting impacts a text's direction. For example, how is the storyline affected by the time and location of the story's events?

Recurring Themes

Texts may carry recurring themes like acceptance, courage, loyalty, man versus nature, family, and life. There are many themes that may overlap in a variety of texts. It is important for teachers to remember to coordinate texts with recurring themes in order for students to clearly understand the intent or message.

Style and Figurative Language

Inferential reading and comprehension skills, such as figurative language, involve some abstract understanding of the text. Students must first gain comprehension of the text, and then use their inference skills to further break down the text. Students must understand characters' feelings as well as the reason for the setting. Again, identifying theme is a difficult skill to teach. When introducing a new text, teachers should provide students with a list of common themes to pick from. Figurative language and literary devices can help identify the theme. **Figurative language** includes metaphors, similes, personification, and hyperbole. **Literary devices** include imagery, symbolism, irony, and foreshadowing. These two tools help readers interpret the author's theme or purpose in texts.

Reading Comprehension Strategies for Nonfiction

Informational, Descriptive, and Persuasive Materials

It is important for students to be exposed to a variety of texts, reading materials, and resources. To become well-rounded readers, teachers should provide students with expository texts in addition to the classroom textbooks. Key characteristics of informational and expository texts include informative facts about a specific topic. Since these are nonfiction texts, diagrams or other graphic aids may be used to assist in understanding the text. Other forms of informational text include news articles, research journals, educational magazines with informational text, and websites. These texts can be used in small groups or can be introduced in whole group instruction, and then further explored in small intervention groups.

Fact-based understanding and the use of textual evidence is imperative in expository and informational texts. Students should be able to compare and contrast two different texts and identify problems and solutions as well as cause and effect. Graphic organizers arranged chronologically can help students take notes when covering nonfiction texts. Students need to have the correct order of events in a nonfiction piece in order to identify the cause of an event, as well as the effect it had on problems and solutions. At times, students may need to compare and contrast two texts to identify the similarity of facts, the differences in reported facts, or note any bias from the author. Using knowledge of writing standards and instruction can aid students' understanding of informational text. When comprehending an informative text's objective, students should utilize their prior knowledge of the topic, prior writing assignments, and concluding sentences in the text. This is another example of how reading comprehension and writing go hand-in-hand in the learning process, and how writing and language become important to student comprehension.

Reading Comprehension Strategies

Organizational/Explanatory Features

Using and understanding references is imperative in developing reading comprehension skills. Pre-teaching a lesson on understanding references can be helpful, or a teacher may even incorporate this skill into teaching some broader comprehension skills. Prior to teaching from the basal reader, or prior to each story in the basal reader, a teacher should address the table of contents at the beginning of the textbook. This teaches students to use the table of contents frequently and allows them to find parts of a story that they will be reading on their own. When teaching from nonfiction texts, such as social studies or science, instruction should be provided on using the index to identify and locate specific information to answer comprehension questions. Both nonfiction and fiction texts can be used to teach how to use the glossary to locate boldfaced and important vocabulary. It is often most beneficial to identify and teach new vocabulary prior to reading a piece, so that students gain a deeper understanding of the text as they read it for the first time.

Typographic Features

Understanding changes in the appearance of text will help students easily identify important information. Pointing out boldfaced words during reading instruction tells students these may be important words in the understanding of the text, and that new vocabulary may be present. Boldfacing or italics may help students identify when a thought or topic is changing or being brought to attention. Color-coding may be used when comparing or contrasting different parts of the text. During reading comprehension instruction time, it is important to point out when these changes occur. It is also helpful to try to find text of this nature to use in small group or whole group instruction. Text with these types of typographic features assist students on their path to reading comprehension.

Graphic Features

Graphics always help interpret a story or text. Younger learners rely on pictures to help tell the story, while older students use diagrams, maps, and charts to aid in understanding texts. Even for adults, graphic features assist with visualizing the text being read. Charts and diagrams help organize information into more clear and concise patterns. Maps help understand specific places and locations. Illustrations help visualize a fictional story. Furthermore, illustrations with captions help visualize nonfiction and fiction texts, particularly when paired with captions that provide an explanation of why the illustration is important.

Main Ideas, Supporting Details, and Author's Purpose

Topics and main ideas are critical parts of any writing. The **topic** is the subject matter of the piece, and it is a broader, more general term. The **main idea** is what the writer wants to say about that topic. The topic can be expressed in a word or two, but the main idea should be a complete thought.

The topic and main idea are usually easy to recognize in nonfiction writing. An author will likely identify the topic immediately in the first sentence of a passage or essay. The main idea is also typically presented in the introductory paragraph of an essay. In a single passage, the main idea may be identified in the first or the last sentence, but will likely be directly stated and easily recognized by the reader.

Because it is not always stated immediately in a passage, it's important to carefully read the entire passage to identify the main idea.

Readers should also remember that when most authors write, they want to make a point or send a message. This point or message of a text is known as the **theme**. Authors may state themes explicitly, like in *Aesop's Fables*. More often, especially in modern literature, readers must infer the theme based on text details. Usually after carefully reading and analyzing an entire text, the theme emerges. Typically, the longer the piece, the more themes the reader will encounter, though often one theme dominates the rest, as evidenced by the author's purposeful revisiting of it throughout the passage.

The main idea should not be confused with the thesis statement. A **thesis statement** is a clear statement of the writer's specific stance, and can often be found in the introduction of a nonfiction piece. The main idea is more of an overview of the entire piece, while the thesis is a specific sentence found in that piece.

In order to illustrate the main idea, a writer will use **supporting details** in a passage. These details can provide evidence or examples to help make a point. Supporting details are most commonly found in nonfiction pieces that seek to inform or persuade the reader.

A reader should carefully examine the author's supporting details to be sure they are credible. The reader needs to consider whether the supporting details provide evidence of the author's point and whether they directly support the main idea. Readers might find that an author has used a shocking statistic to grab their attention, but that the statistic doesn't really support the main idea, so it isn't being effectively used in the piece.

Logical Organization and Structural Patterns in Nonfiction Text

Structural Patterns of a Text

Teaching students text structure helps them to search for information when answering questions about the text. This again integrates reading and writing strategies when learning about comprehension. Text needs should be written in a logical way. Consistent and logical written thoughts aid in comprehension and help readers find information easier within the text, especially when trying to locate answers to comprehension questions. Students should recall that the broader meaning of text is located at the beginning of a story, and more specific details are provided throughout the text. Subtitles will help students locate information they are seeking.

Local Organization

Nonfiction is inherently different from fiction, both in context and structure. Students will find that nonfiction lacks the metaphors, similes, and artistic structures of poetry or literature that are used to deliver symbolic meaning. This might seem daunting to them at first. However, this is something easily overcome by careful analysis of the local organization within the nonfiction text in question.

Instructors can point out that, unlike fiction, nonfiction does not embed the main point or meaning of the text within a narrative or through artistic word choices but clearly presents the central theme. This makes the author's intention more direct and clear and is done through a variety of methods depending on the voice and goals of the reader. When reading nonfiction, instructors should have the students look for clues indicating what the author is saying and objectives behind what's being said. Is the author seeking to argue a point, disprove a point, or simply educate the reader? Asking these questions will help the students look at how the text is organized to find these answers.

Instructors must clarify that nonfiction writing revolves around a central idea and supporting information. Students can point out the central idea by looking at the opening of the text to see if there are any direct statements or a question presented. Throughout the reading, instructors can ask students if there are recurring statements or ideas. Does the author return to an initial statement/idea? Or is the author simply writing information? If the author keeps returning to a key statement, it may indicate that their focus is on this idea. From here, the structure of supporting information will reveal even more.

Supporting information fills the majority of the nonfiction text. If the author is just reflecting on something, students should note how the author populates the text with details or how and why they think a certain way. Alternatively, if the author is trying to prove a point, the information will present and explain evidence to corroborate their claim. Some of the patterns for organizing information include sequence, cause and effect, compare and contrast, description, and problem and solution. Having students identify and group the supporting information into one of these categories will help them grasp the author's motive and gain insight from the overall piece.

Using Evidence from Nonfiction Texts

Literal and Figurative Meanings

It is important when evaluating informational texts to consider the use of both literal and figurative meanings. The words and phrases an author chooses to include in a text must be evaluated. How does the word choice affect the meaning and tone? By recognizing the use of literal and figurative language, a reader can more readily ascertain the message or purpose of a text. **Literal** word choice is the easiest to analyze as it represents the usual and intended way a word or phrase is used. It is also more common in informational texts because it is used to state facts and definitions. While **figurative language** is typically associated with fiction and poetry, it can be found in informational texts as well. The reader must determine not only what is meant by the figurative language in context, but also how the author intended it to shape the overall text.

Inferences in Informational Texts

Inference refers to the reader's ability to understand the unwritten text, i.e., "read between the lines" in terms of an author's intent or message. The strategy asks that a reader not take everything he or she reads at face value but instead, add his or her own interpretation of what the author seems to be trying to convey. A reader's ability to make inferences relies on his or her ability to think clearly and logically about the text. It does not ask that the reader make wild speculations or guess about the material but demands that he or she be able to come to a sound conclusion about the material.

An author's use of less literal words and phrases requires readers to make more inference when they read. Since inference involves **deduction**—deriving conclusions from ideas assumed to be true—there's more room for interpretation. Still, critical readers who employ inference, if careful in their thinking, can arrive at the logical, sound conclusions the author intends.

Questioning has immeasurable value in the reading process. Answering questions about a text gives purpose for reading to students and focuses them on reading to learn information. Similarly, generating questions about a text for others to answer enables a student to analyze what is important to learn in the text and glean summarizing skills. Keeping s's Taxonomy in mind, teachers can scaffold students toward increased critical thinking capabilities. Bloom's Taxonomy shows the hierarchy of learning progressing through the following stages:

- Remembering
- Understanding
- Applying
- Analyzing
- Evaluating
- Creating

Textual Evidence in Informational Text

Once a reader has determined an author's thesis or main idea, he or she will need to understand how textual evidence supports interpretation of that thesis or main idea. Test takers will be asked direct questions regarding an author's main idea and may be asked to identify evidence that would support those ideas. This will require test takers to comprehend literal and figurative meanings within the text passage, be able to draw inferences from provided information, and be able to separate important evidence from minor supporting detail. It's often helpful to skim test questions and answer options prior to critically reading informational text; however, test takers should avoid the temptation to solely look for the correct answers. Just trying to find the "right answer" may cause test takers to miss important supporting textual evidence. Making a mental note of test questions is only helpful as a guide when reading.

After identifying an author's thesis or main idea, a test taker should look at the supporting details that the author provides to back up his or her assertions, identifying those additional pieces of information that help expand the thesis. From there, test takers should examine the additional information and related details for credibility, the author's use of outside sources, and be able to point to direct evidence that supports the author's claims. It's also imperative that test takers be able to identify what is strong support and what is merely additional information that is nice to know but not necessary. Being able to make this differentiation will help test takers effectively answer questions regarding an author's use of supporting evidence within informational text.

Writing Skills and Processes

Writing as a Developmental Process

Almost all coherent written works contain three primary parts: a beginning, middle, and end. The organizational arrangements differ widely across distinct writing modes. Persuasive and expository texts utilize an introduction, body, and conclusion whereas narrative works use an orientation, series of events/conflict, and a resolution.

Every element within a written piece relates back to the main idea, and the beginning of a persuasive or expository text generally conveys the main idea or the purpose. For a narrative piece, the beginning is the section that acquaints the reader with the characters and setting, directing them to the purpose of the writing. The main idea in narrative may be implied or addressed at the end of the piece.

Depending on the primary purpose, the arrangement of the middle will adhere to one of the basic organizational structures described in the information texts and rhetoric section. They are cause and effect, problem and solution, compare and contrast, description/spatial, sequence, and order of importance.

The ending of a text is the metaphorical wrap-up of the writing. A solid ending is crucial for effective writing as it ties together loose ends, resolves the action, highlights the main points, or repeats the central idea. A **conclusion** ensures that readers come away from a text understanding the author's main idea. The table below highlights the important characteristics of each part of a piece of writing.

Structure	Argumentative/Informative	Narrative
Beginning	Introduction Purpose, main idea	Orientation Introduces characters, setting, necessary background
Middle	Body Supporting details, reasons, and evidence	Events/Conflict Story's events that revolve around a central conflict
End	Conclusion Highlights main points, summarizes and paraphrases ideas, reiterates the main idea	Resolution The solving of the central conflict

Writing in Various Forms

Distinguishing Between Common Modes of Writing

To distinguish between the common modes of writing, it is important to identify the primary purpose of the work. This can be determined by considering what the author is trying to say to the reader. Although there are countless different styles of writing, all written works tend to fall under four primary categories: argumentative/persuasive, informative expository, descriptive, and narrative.

The table below highlights the purpose, distinct characteristics, and examples of each rhetorical mode:

Writing Mode	Purpose	Distinct Characteristics	Examples
Argumentative	To persuade	Opinions, loaded or subjective language, evidence, suggestions of what the reader should do, calls to action	Critical reviews Political journals Letters of recommendation Cover letters Advertising
Informative	To teach or inform	Objective language, definitions, instructions, factual information	Business and scientific reports Textbooks Instruction manuals News articles Personal letters Wills Informative essays Travel guides Study guides
Descriptive	To deliver sensory details to the reader	Heavy use of adjectives and imagery, language that appeals to any of the five senses	Poetry Journal entries Often used in narrative mode
Narrative	To tell a story, share an experience, or entertain	Series of events, plot, characters, dialogue, conflict	Novels Short stories Novellas Anecdotes Biographies Epic poems Autobiographies

Promoting Writing Skills

Writing is an important component in literacy development. Writing is the next phase in reading comprehension. This level may include summarizing (especially in the younger grade levels), outlining, and responding to questions. Once a student can analyze a text and orally respond, he or she can then write his or her response on paper. New standards require written responses to texts; the new Common Core standards are putting greater emphasis on written responses. Students are required to answer comprehension questions with a written response style, as opposed to the traditional selected-response style used in the past. Students need to be able to outline and create notes on a text while reading it. In this way, students have the ability to respond to comprehension questions while referencing their outlines. Outlines should include important points, page numbers, and perhaps even paragraph numbers. Students can also use graphic organizers to outline and summarize the text. Writing is shown to enhance comprehension and memory. Simply having students write about what they are reading reinforces text comprehension.

6+1 Traits Strategy for Teaching Writing

6+1 Traits is a model for teaching writing that uses a common language to explain the standards for what good writing looks like. Students learn to evaluate whether these expectations have been met in their own writing and then edit, revise, and rewrite accordingly. The 6+1 Traits are the characteristics that make writing readable and effective no matter what genre of writing is being used. The 6+1 Traits are as follows:

- Ideas
- Organization
- Voice
- Word choice
- Sentence fluency
- Conventions
- Presentation

6+1 traits of writing

The Ideas Trait
This trait is the content of the writing. This is where students learn to select an important topic for their writing. They are taught to narrow down and focus their idea. Then they learn to develop and elaborate on the specific idea. Finally, they investigate and discover the information and details that best convey the idea to others.

The Organization Trait
This trait teaches students how to build the framework for their writing. They choose an organizational strategy or purpose for the writing and build the details upon that structure. There are many purposes for writing, and they all have different frameworks. However, there are commonalities that students can learn to effectively organize their writing so it makes sense to the reader. Students learn to invite the reader into their work with an effective introduction. They are taught how to create thoughtful transitions between ideas and key points in their writing and how to create logical and purposeful sequencing of ideas. Finally, students are taught how to create a powerful conclusion to their piece that summarizes the information but leaves the reader with something to think about. Many students are inclined to jump into their writing without a clear direction for where it is going. The organization trait teaches them to plan and purpose their writing toward excellence.

The Voice Trait
This is the trait that gives the writing a sense of individuality and connection to the author. It shows that the writing is meaningful and that the author cares about it. It is what makes the writing uniquely the author's own. It is how the reader begins to know the author and what she or he "sounds like." Students learn to recognize "voice" in some writing samples and find their own "voice" to apply to their work. Students are taught to speak on an emotional level directly to their readers. Students experiment with matching their style to the audience and the purpose of the writing. Students are taught to enjoy taking risks and putting their personal touch into their work.

The Word Choice Trait
This trait gives writing a sense of functional communication through precise language that is rich and enlightening. If the work is narrative, the words create images in the mind's eye; if the work is descriptive, the words clarify and expand thoughts and ideas. If the work is persuasive, the words give new perspective and invite thought. Students learn not only to choose exceptional vocabulary, but also to hone their skills for using ordinary words well. Students are taught to describe things using striking language. They learn to use exact language that is accurate, concise, precise, and lively.

62

The Sentence Fluency Trait

When sentences are built to fit together and move with one another to create writing that is easy to read aloud, the author has written with fluency. Students learn to eliminate awkward word patterns that otherwise would encumber the reader. Sentences and paragraphs start and stop in precisely the right places so that the writing moves well. Students are taught to establish a flow, develop a rhythm, and give cadence to their work. They edit their sentences to vary the structure and length. Educators can teach fluency through reading aloud beautifully written examples and contrasting them with less fluent work.

The Conventions Trait

Here the focus changes from creation of the piece to preparation for the reader. Instead of revision that the first five traits teach, this trait teaches editing skills. The students learn to make their writing clear and understandable through the use of proper grammar, spelling, capitalization, and punctuation. Students are taught the differences between revision and editing. They learn basic editing marks and symbols. Teachers can assist students to learn conventions through guided editing and regular practice. Expectations for correctness need to be kept developmentally appropriate. If immediate correctness is expected, students may shy away from experimenting and taking risks.

The Presentation Trait

This trait focuses on the final appearance of the work. Presentation is not a concern during the process of the other six traits, nor must perfect presentation be expected for every work a student does. Students are taught to make their work inviting and accessible to the reader of the end product. They learn to show they care about their writing when it is neat and readable. Students are taught about uniform spacing, legible handwriting, appropriate use of fonts and sizes, and how to use bullets, numbers, headings, charts, graphs, and pictures to help make the work visually appealing. Students are taught about the publishing process and are given opportunities to showcase their finished products.

Recursive Stages in the Writing Process

Like with any complicated processes, writing development begins with the simplest form of indiscernible scribbles and progresses to fully formed words and, finally, to clearly written sentences and paragraphs. This is actually a complicated cognitive process that takes time and instruction to improve.

With very young students, emphasis can focus on simply making letters clear. After all, letters and word formation are the starting blocks of written language. The next phase in development can focus on actually creating words and making sure they are spelled correctly. When students are at the sentence development stage, grammar and linguistic rules become a priority. The foundations of the English language need to be firm in order for students to have good writing. When students have progressed to more advanced levels and are composing fully formed sentences with a specific purpose, it's time to incorporate content-related feedback.

Feedback at all levels of writing development is crucial; this is how students will learn to correct mistakes and strengthen growing skills. Instructor feedback must be clear while also being sensitive to the students' struggles or backgrounds. Differentiated instruction may be required to bolster students' writing skills. A good starting point for overall writing instruction is to introduce students to the stages of writing an original piece.

The goal with the stages of writing is to build on the previous work. The prewriting stage is the time for students to just write down ideas and plan on how they will approach the topic at hand. The actual writing stage then dovetails on this fluidly because the student already has a framework of what the writing will focus on and how they will present information. In addition to practicing physical writing, these stages focus on critical-thinking and planning skills and may lessen the student's stress before they write and receive feedback. Feedback on the initial writing, or first draft, is key. The instructor should be able to assess any difficulties and then steer the student toward improving their writing in the revision stage. After revisions, instructors should examine how effective their feedback was in helping the writing improve overall.

Effective Composing

Good writing is composed of several key elements: development, focus, clarity and coherence, grammatical proficiency, and originality. Different institutions and individual instructors will list such qualities differently, but good composition will have these basic qualities.

Strong compositions have well-developed ideas that are explained clearly throughout the piece. Good writing seems to have been planned and executed without any gaps or confusion. Through their writing, students must essentially develop an idea and line of reasoning that leave readers clear about the focus of the piece. This also means that paragraphs must be arranged in a way that they enhance and expand on the central focus of the paper, using evidence sensibly.

A writer's focus is the central point. A successful composition will not only contain a clear focus but carry the focus throughout the piece. The reader should never lose the focus or be confused by it. The way in which the content is presented throughout the text, while remaining focused on the central idea, is key. This is done by the tactical use of evidence surrounding and supporting claims relating to the central idea.

Language can be elegant and creative, but it must be used in a way the reader can understand. Much of a writer's success will depend on the coherence of the written piece. Paragraphs and the ideas within them should not be random but connect together, seamlessly blending into the next section to advance the focus of the writing. Each paragraph should strengthen the claim. Unnecessary paragraphs disrupt the flow of the writing and distract the reader, ultimately weakening the piece. Naturally, the writing should also be grammatically correct and proofed for accurate spelling and sentence structure.

Originality is the defining aspect of a well-written piece. Students should not parrot the writing style or ideas of others but instead write something that is unique. Ideas, and the way they are presented, should be fresh and approach topics in a way that offers a new perspective to the reader.

Effective Written Expression

Written expression refers to the ability of the writer to fluidly communicate meaning and purpose throughout the composition. Essentially, this refers not only to how clear the central focus of the piece is but how well the ideas surrounding the central focus are presented. If the writer can't successfully express the meaning and implications of the idea, the writing will not be strong.

Effective written expression utilizes detailed, clear communication. A writer doesn't need to unload elaborate diction throughout the paragraphs. Such an embellishment can be distracting to the reader, which actually defeats the principles behind effective writing. Sentences should be direct and emphasize language that, while engaging, remains simple enough for the audience to understand. This doesn't mean abstaining from using advanced words but rather keeping sentences direct and to the point. Students should avoid rambling line after line. Avoiding exaggerating language or overdramatic phrasing is also important. Not only can this confuse the reader, it can also harm the reader's credibility.

A simple formula for effective writing is to introduce an idea, discuss it, and then make a conclusion. This applies for the written piece as a whole but must also be used within individual paragraphs. If a writer just introduces idea after idea with no substance, the reader is left with unsubstantiated claims. Without supporting evidence to understand the view, the reader is left with only opinion. With the implementation of facts and supporting details, this opinion is strengthened. Thus, the reasoning behind the central idea is clearly executed and can be considered seriously. This helps the writer achieve credibility.

Paragraph coherence is vital for effective written expression. Paragraph sequencing and information placement are essential to streamlining the entire piece. Evidence and supporting information should be used to transition from one section to another, up to the conclusion. This enables the information to be clearly expressed. The author should strive to write in a way that, as the piece progresses, the focus becomes clearer and more convincing. By the conclusion of the written piece, the author should also restate his or her thesis to solidify their views and reasoning.

Interdependence of Reading and Writing Development

The goal of sight word instruction is to help students readily recognize regular and irregular high-frequency words in order to aid reading fluency and comprehension. Several factors affect the sequence of instruction for specific sight words. For example, before a child is exposed to sight words, he or she needs to be able to fluently recognize and say the sound of all uppercase and lowercase letters. Also, students need to be able to accurately decode target words before they recognize sight words. When irregular words are introduced, attention should be drawn to both the phonetically regular and the phonetically irregular portions of the words.

Before sight word instruction can begin, teachers need to identify high-frequency words that do and do not follow normal spelling conventions, but are used often. Teachers may choose to select words that are used often within their students' reading materials, words that students have an interest in learning, or content-specific words. Alternatively, grade-level standardized sight word lists, such as the Dolch word lists, can be referenced.

Repetition and exposure through guided and independent practice are essential in student retention of sight words. Each lesson should introduce only three to five new sight words and also review words from previous lessons. Visually similar words should not be introduced in proximity to one another.

Sample activities through which sight words can be taught are listed below.

1. Students can practice reading decodable texts and word lists.

2. Teachers should read text that contains the sight words that a class is currently learning. As a teacher reads aloud, they should pause, point to, and correctly pronounce the words. Instead of pointing to the words, teachers can underline or highlight the words as they appear in sentences that are read.

3. Flashcards can be used to practice sight word recognition.

4. Games are fun and motivating avenues through which sight words can be practiced. Examples of games that can be used to practice sight words include Bingo, Go Fish, and Memory.

5. As students learn new sight words, they can write them in a sight word "dictionary." Students should be asked to write a sentence using each sight word included within the dictionary.

The spelling of high-frequency words should be taught after students have been exposed to the words, can readily recognize the words, and can read the words. The following multisensory strategies can be used to help students master the spelling of high-frequency sight words:

1. Spell Reading: Spell reading begins when a student says the high-frequency word. Then, the student spells out the letters in the word. Lastly, the student reads the word again. Spell reading helps commit the word to a student's memory when done in repetition.

2. Air Writing: When air writing, a student uses their finger to write the letters of a word in the air.

3. Arm Tapping: During arm tapping, a student says the word, spells the word's letters on their arm, and then reads the word again.

4. Table Writing: Students write the word on the table. A substrate, where the word is written in sand or shaving cream, can be added to the table. See examples of substrates below:

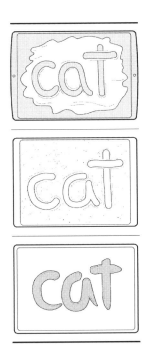

5. Letter Magnet Spelling: Arranging letter magnets on a metal surface, such as a cookie sheet, is a fun way for students to learn how to spell sight words. Because this strategy is seen as a game to the student, letter magnet spelling increases student motivation to write words.

6. Material Writing: Students can use clay, play dough, Wikki sticks, or other materials to form letters that are used to spell the words.

Correct Spelling, Usage, and Other Writing Mechanics

Spelling as a Developmental Process

Decoding and encoding are reciprocal phonological skills, meaning that the steps to each are opposite of one another.

Decoding is the application of letter-sound correspondences, letter patterns, and other phonics relationships that help students read and correctly pronounce words. Decoding helps students to recognize and read words quickly, increasing reading fluency and comprehension. The order of the steps that occur during the decoding process are as follows:

1. The student identifies a written letter or letter combination.

2. The student makes correlations between the sound of the letter or sounds of the letter combination.

3. The student understands how the letters or letter combinations fit together.

4. The student verbally blends the letter and letter combinations together to form a word.

Encoding is the spelling of words. In order to properly spell words, students must be familiar with letter/sound correspondences. Students must be able to put together phonemes, digraphs or blends, morphological units, consonant/vowel patterns, etc. The steps of encoding are identified below:

1. The student understands that letters and sounds make up words.

2. The student segments the sound parts of a word.

3. The student identifies the letter or letter combinations that correspond to each sound part.

4. The student then writes the letters and letter combinations in order to create the word.

Because the stages of decoding and spelling are essentially opposite of one another, they are reciprocal skills. Thus, phonics knowledge supports the development of reading and spelling. Likewise, the development of spelling knowledge reinforces phonics and decoding knowledge. In fact, the foundation of all good spelling programs is their alignment to reading instruction and a student's reading level.

Because of the reciprocal relationship between decoding and encoding, the development of phonics, vocabulary, and spelling are interrelated. The instruction of phonics begins with simple syllable patterns. Phonics instruction then progresses toward more difficult syllable patterns, more complex phonics patterns, the sounds of morphemes, and strategies for decoding multisyllabic words. Through this process, new vocabulary is developed. Sight word instruction should not begin until students are able to decode target words with automaticity and accuracy. Spelling is the last instructional component to be introduced.

Spelling development occurs in stages. In order, these stages are the pre-phonetic stage, the semiphonetic stage, the phonetic stage, the transitional stage, and the conventional stage. Each stage is explained below. Ways in which phonics and vocabulary development fit into the spelling stages are discussed. Instructional strategies for each phase of spelling are suggested.

Spelling development begins with the **pre-phonetic stage.** This stage is marked by an incomplete understanding of the alphabetic principle. Student understanding of letter-sound correspondences is limited. During the pre-phonetic stage, students participate in precommunicative writing. **Precommunicative writing** appears to be a jumble of letter-like forms rather than a series of discrete letters. Students' precommunicative writing samples can be used as informal assessments of their understanding of the alphabetic principle and knowledge of letter-sound correspondences.

Pre-phonetic stage of spelling development

The pre-phonetic stage is followed by the **semiphonetic stage**. In this stage, a student understands that letters represent sounds. The alphabetic principle may be understood, but letter recognition may not yet be fully developed. In this stage, single letters may be used to represent entire words (e.g., *U* for *you*). Other times, multiple syllables within words may be omitted. Writing produced by students in this stage is still virtually unreadable. Teachers may ask students to provide drawings to supplement their writing to better determine what a student intended to write.

Semiphonetc stage of writing

The third stage in spelling development is the **phonetic stage**. In this stage, students have mastered letter-sound correspondences. Although letters may be written backward or upside down, phonetic spellers are able to write all of the letters in the alphabet. Because phonetic spellers have limited sight vocabulary, irregular words are often spelled incorrectly. However, words that are written may phonetically sound like the spoken word. Additionally, student writing becomes systematic. For example, students are likely to use one letter to represent a digraph or letter blend (e.g., *f* for /ph/).

Phonetic stage of writing

Spelling instruction of common consonant patterns, short vowel sounds, and common affixes or rimes can begin during the phonetic stage. Thus, spelling instruction during the phonetic stage coincides with the instruction of phonics and phonemic awareness that also occurs during this stage of development.

The creation of word walls is advantageous during the phonetic stage of spelling development. On a word wall, words that share common consonant-vowel patterns or letter clusters are written in groups. Students are encouraged to add words to the group. As a result, word walls promote strategic spelling, vocabulary development, common letter combinations, and common morphological units.

The **transitional stage** of spelling occurs when a student has developed a small sight vocabulary and a solid understanding of letter-sound correspondences. Thus, spelling dependence on phonology decreases. Instead, dependence on visual representation and word structure increases. As sight word vocabulary increases during the transition stage, the correct spelling of irregular words will also increase. However, students may still struggle to spell words with long vowel sounds.

Transitional stage of spelling

Differentiation of spelling instruction often begins during the transitional stage. Instruction ought to be guided by data collected through informal observations and informal assessments. Depending on individual needs, lessons may include sight word recognition, morphology, etymology, reading, and writing. It is during the transitional stage that the instruction of homophones can begin. **Homophones** are words that sound the same but have different spellings and meanings (e.g., *their* and *there*). Additionally, students should be expected to begin writing full sentences at the transitional stage. Writing will not only reinforce correct spelling of words but also phonics and vocabulary development.

Conventional spelling is the last and final stage of spelling development. This stage occurs after a student's sight word vocabulary recognition is well developed and the student is able to read fluently and with comprehension. By this stage, students know the basic rules of phonics. They are able to deal with consonants, multiple vowel-consonant blends, homophones, digraphs, and irregular spellings. Due to an increase in sight word recognition at this stage, a conventional speller is able to recognize when a word is spelled incorrectly.

It is at the conventional spelling stage that spelling instruction can begin to focus on content-specific vocabulary words and words with unusual spellings. In order to further reinforce vocabulary development of such content-specific words and apply phonic skills, students should be encouraged to use the correct spelling of such words within various writing activities.

For even the best conventional spellers, some words will still cause consistent trouble. Students can keep track of words that they consistently spell incorrectly or find confusing in word banks so they can isolate and eventually eliminate their individualized errors. Students can use their word banks as references when they come across a word with which they struggle. Students may also spend time consciously committing the words in their banks to memory through verbal or written practice.

Conventional stage

Systematic Spelling Instruction

As students become more advanced in their decoding abilities, they will begin to read words that are increasingly more complex linguistically. Teachers should continue using decodable text so that students can continue practicing phonics elements and sight words already taught.

Whole-to-part instruction can be used with students who display more advanced decoding abilities. During whole-to-part instruction, a sentence, a word, and then a sound-symbol relationship is the focus of instruction. Additionally, CVCC, CCVC, and CVVC words that contain common and regular letter combinations can be taught as well as regular CVCe words. Teachers can begin introducing less common phonics elements, such as *kn* or *ph*. It is during this stage that students are taught how to add common inflected endings or suffixes (*-ed, -er, -est, -ing,* etc.) to single-syllable base words.

Finally, phonics knowledge is used to spell more complex orthographic patterns in single-syllable words. **Orthography** is the study of a language's spelling conventions. Orthography includes the rules of spelling, hyphenation, capitalization, pronunciation, emphasis, and word breaks. Orthographic processing requires students to use their visual systems to envision, store, recall, and form words.

The prescribed teaching sequence of orthographic patterns is found in the next chart.

Orthographic Pattern	Example of Pattern
Awareness of letter-sound correspondences	Understanding that each letter has a certain sound as well as a name
Understanding that letters form words	Recoding certain CVC words like *dog, hug,* and *jar*
Simple consonant blends and matching sound patterns	Recognizing onsets and rimes of single-syllable words like *cat* as *c-at* and *star* as *st-ar*
Recognizing single-syllable words	Uses CVC, CCVC, or CVCC patterns
Ability to read more complex consonant blends	Reading and recognizing single-syllable words like *cross, lamp,* and *track*
Long versus short vowels	Identifying words that contain long and short vowel sounds
Vowel-Vowel and Vowel-Consonant Digraphs	Identifying words like *whey, tree,* and *phone*
Vowel-Vowel Digraphs that have the same sound	Identifying sounds such as /ay/, /ai/, or /a-e/
Vowel-Consonant Digraphs can be associated with different sounds	Identifying words like *cool* versus *boot, harm* versus *hare,* etc.
Complex single-syllable digraphs and trigraphs	Introducing the *tch* trigraph
Syllabication	Ability to split words into syllables
"Silent Letters" within words	Identifying words that contain silent letters such as *write, knock,* or *plumb*
Blending of two-syllable words	Reading two-syllable words such as *stumble, candle,* etc.
Morphemes within two-syllable words	Identifying correct syllabication of two-syllable words like *post-pone* versus *po-stpone*
Meaning of morphemes	An example would be knowing "macro" means "large" or "great"
Understanding letter clusters	Identifying that the "s" at the end of a word means its plural, and that the "ed" at the end of a word means it's in past tense.
Syllabication of nonconventional morphemes with multisyllabic words	Syllabication of morphemes that are not pronounced how they are written, like *ance* or *tion.*

Writing Mechanics

Educators must first be masters of the English language in order to teach it. Teachers serve several key roles in the classroom that all require that they know the conventions of grammar, punctuation, and spelling. Teachers are communicators. They must know how to structure their own language for clarity. They must also be able to interpret what the students are saying to accurately either affirm or revise it for correctness. Teachers are educators of language. They are the agents of change from poor-quality conventions to mastery of the concepts. Teachers are responsible for differentiating instruction so that students at all levels and aptitudes can succeed with language learning. Teachers need to be able to isolate gaps in skill sets and decide which skills need intervention in the classroom.

Teachers are evaluators. They are responsible for making key decisions about a student's educational trajectory based on their assessment of the student's capabilities.

Teachers also have great impact on how students view themselves as learners. Teachers are models. They must be superb examples of educated individuals. Just like with any other subject, people need a strong grasp of the basics of language. They will not be able to learn these things unless the teachers themselves have mastered it.

Teachers foster socialization; socialization to cultural norms and to the everyday practices of the community in which they live is of utmost importance to students' lives. These processes begin at home but continue early in a child's life at school. Teachers play a key role in guiding and scaffolding students' socialization skills. If teachers are to excel in this role, they need to be adept with the use of the English language.

Teachers need to have mastery of the conventions of English including:

- Nouns
- Collective Nouns
- Compound Subjects
- Pronouns
- Subjects, Objects, and Compounds
- Pronoun/Noun Agreement
- Indefinite Pronouns
- Choosing Pronouns
- Adjectives
- Compound Adjectives
- Verbs
- Infinitives
- Verb Tenses
- Participles
- Subject/Verb Agreement
- Active/Passive Voice
- Adverbs
- Double Negatives
- Comparisons
- Double Comparisons
- Prepositions
- Prepositional Phrases
- Conjunctions
- Interjections
- Articles
- Types of sentences
- Subjects and Predicates
- Clauses and Phrases
- Pronoun Reference Problems
- Misplaced Modifiers
- Dangling Participial Phrases

- Punctuation
- Periods
- Commas
- Semicolons and Colons
- Parentheses and Dashes
- Quotation Marks
- Apostrophes
- Hyphens
- Question Marks
- Exclamation Points
- Capitalization
- Spelling
- Noun Plurals
- Prefixes and Suffixes
- Spelling Hurdles
- Abbreviations
- Pronunciation
- Homonyms and other easy mix-ups

Writing and Reading as Tools for Inquiry and Research

Promoting Research Skills

Classrooms are utilizing more demanding research skills and projects. Science experiments and invention fairs encourage students to develop their own questions and topics to explore through research. Students should select topics that they want to research, apply, and solve. This can then be developed into academic arguments, which counter previous findings on a topic. When evaluating a topic, students can research and explore the topic while using their previous understanding of comparing and contrasting various texts.

With the increased reliance on technology in classrooms, at home, and in all facets of daily life, schools are encouraging the use of technology in lessons. Even in the primary grades, teachers are assigning more research-based projects to introduce technology to students at an early age. This way, when students reach higher grade levels, their previous understanding of how and where to find information to answer questions and summarize information can be developed even further. The older grades incorporate using multiple sources, asking and evaluating questions, and thinking of their own research topics to explore. This development of instructional strategies and research skills proves to be beneficial in the sciences as well as the new generation of S.T.E.M. learning. Again, reading comprehension skills are essential to the development of research skills.

Text Organizers

Organizing information is one of the core components of competent writing. The better an essay is organized, the clearer and more engaging it will be to read. It's important for instructors to emphasize information analysis and its use in structuring writing effectively. Categorizing information enables students to understand what kind of details the information presents and then use those details to effectively strengthen their argument or narrative.

One method of organizing information is to simply present it in **chronological order**, a straightforward sequence that builds on events or discoveries to illustrate a passage of time to the reader. If students are writing about historical events, for example, grouping details chronologically makes the most sense. The writer will be able to lead the reader through a defined order as opposed to going back and forth between details. Just as everyone experiences time from past, to present, to future, the reader will be able to relate to and follow the text details with ease.

Grouping related or common themed information within the writing is also highly effective. If there are significant portions of a composition focusing on one aspect of the evidence, a specific event, or analyzing a certain source, writers should keep these concentrated areas together. If one section of the writing shifts from one focal point to another but then back to the first, it will cause confusion and disrupt the writing flow. Grouping related information will help the writing make logical sense and also show the depth of the topic that is the focus.

Sometimes it can be useful to have information located in a way that facts or viewpoints are compared and contrasted. If used incorrectly, details meant to strengthen a paper's position may weaken it. However, when used correctly, comparing and contrasting relevant details can enhance a writer's argument. Readers also gain more context to understand the full scope of the topic. If a compare-and-contrast section is used, students must address not only the reasons for this structure, but also show how these details support the main point.

Reference Materials

Reference materials are indispensable tools for beginners and experts alike. Becoming a competent English communicator doesn't necessarily mean memorizing every single rule about spelling, grammar, or punctuation; rather, it means knowing where and how to find accurate information about the rules of English usage. Students of English have a wide variety of references materials available to them, and, in an increasingly digitized world, more and more of these materials can be found online or as easily-accessible phone applications. Educators should introduce students to different types of reference materials as well as when and how to use them.

Spell Check
Most word processing software programs come equipped with a spell checking feature. Web browsers and personal devices like smartphones and tablets may also have a spell checker enabled. **Spell check** automatically detects misspelled words and suggests alternate spellings. Many writers have come to rely on spell check due to its convenience and ease of use. However, there are some caveats to using spell check—it only checks whether a word is spelled correctly, not if it is used correctly. As discussed above, there are numerous examples of commonly-confused words in English, the misuse of which may not be detected by a spell checker. Many word processing programs do integrate spell checking and grammar checking functions, however. Thus, although running a spell check is an important part of reviewing any piece of writing, it should not be the only step of the review process. Further, spell checkers recommend correctly-spelled words based on an approximation of the misspelled word, so writers need to be somewhat close to the correct spelling in order for spell check to be useful.

Dictionary
Dictionaries are readily available in print, digital formats, and as mobile apps. A dictionary offers a wealth of information to users. First, in the absence of spell checking software, a **dictionary** can be used to identify correct spelling and to determine the word's pronunciation—often written using the International Phonetic Alphabet (IPA). Perhaps the best-known feature of a dictionary is its explanation

of a word's meanings as a single word can have multiple definitions. A dictionary organizes these definitions based on their parts of speech and then arranges them from most to least commonly used meanings or from oldest to most modern usage. Many dictionaries also offer information about a word's etymology and usage. With all these functions, then, a dictionary is a basic, essential tool in many situations. Students can turn to a dictionary when they encounter an unfamiliar word or when they see a familiar word used in a new way.

There are many dictionaries to choose from, but perhaps the most highly respected source is the *Oxford English Dictionary* (OED). The OED is a historical dictionary, and as such, all entries include quotes of the word as it has been used throughout history. Users of the OED can get a deeper sense of a word's evolution over time and in different parts of the world. Another standard dictionary in America is *Merriam-Webster*.

Thesaurus

Whereas a dictionary entry lists a word's definitions, a **thesaurus** entry lists a word's **synonyms** and **antonyms**—i.e., words with similar and opposite meanings, respectively. A dictionary can be used to find out what a word means and where it came from, and a thesaurus can be used to understand a word's relationship to other words. A thesaurus can be a powerful vocabulary-building tool. By becoming familiar with synonyms and antonyms, students will be more equipped to use a broad range of vocabulary in their speech and writing. Of course, one thing to be aware of when using a thesaurus is that most words do not have exact synonyms. Rather, there are slight nuances of meaning that can make one word more appropriate than another in a given context. In this case, it is often to the user's advantage to consult a thesaurus side-by-side with a dictionary to confirm any differences in usage between two synonyms. Some digital sources, such as *Dictionary.com*, integrate a dictionary and a thesaurus.

Generally, though, a thesaurus is a useful tool to help writers add variety and precision to their word choice. Consulting a thesaurus can help students elevate their writing to an appropriate academic level by replacing vague or overused words with more expressive or academic ones. Also, word processors often offer a built-in thesaurus, making it easy for writers to look up synonyms and vary word choice as they work.

Glossary

A **glossary** is similar to a dictionary in that it offers an explanation of terms. However, while a dictionary attempts to cover every word in a language, a glossary only focuses on those terms relevant to a specific field. Also, a glossary entry is more likely to offer a longer explanation of a term and its relevance within that field. Glossaries are often found at the back of textbooks or other nonfiction publications in order to explain new or unfamiliar terms to readers. A glossary may also be an entire book on its own that covers all of the essential terms and concepts within a particular profession, field, or other specialized area of knowledge. Thus, for learners seeking general definitions of terms from any context, a dictionary is an appropriate reference source, but for students of specialized fields, a glossary will usually provide more in-depth information.

Style Manual

Many rules of English usage are standard, but other rules may be more subjective. An example can be seen in the following structures:

    A. I went to the store and bought eggs, milk, and bread.
    B. I went to the store and bought eggs, milk and bread.

The final comma in a list before *and* or *or* is known as an **Oxford comma** or **serial comma**. It is recommended in some styles, but not in others. To determine the appropriate use of the Oxford comma, writers can consult a style manual.

A **style manual** is a comprehensive collection of guidelines for language use and document formatting. Some fields refer to a common style guide—e.g., the Associated Press or *AP Stylebook*, a standard in American journalism. Individual organizations may rely on their own house style. Regardless, the purpose of a style manual is to ensure uniformity across all documents. Style manuals explain things such as how to format titles, when to write out numbers or use numerals, and how to cite sources. Because there are many different style guides, students should know how and when to consult an appropriate guide. *The Chicago Manual of Style* is common in the publication of books and academic journals. The Modern Language Association style (MLA) is another commonly used academic style format, while the American Psychological Association style (APA) may be used for scientific publications. Familiarity with using a style guide is particularly important for students who are college bound or pursuing careers in academic or professional writing.

In the examples above, the Oxford comma is recommended by the Chicago Manual of Style, so sentence A would be correct if the writer is using this style. But the comma is not recommended by the *AP Stylebook*, so sentence B would be correct if the writer is using the AP style.

General Grammar and Style References
Any language arts textbook should offer general grammatical and stylistic advice to students, but there are a few well-respected texts that can also be used for reference. *Elements of Style* by William Strunk is regularly assigned to students as a guide on effective written communication, including how to avoid common usage mistakes and how to make the most of parallel structure. *Garner's Modern American Usage* by Bryan Garner is another text that guides students on how to achieve precision and understandability in their writing. Whereas other reference sources discussed above tend to address specific language concerns, these types of texts offer a more holistic approach to cultivating effective language skills.

Electronic Resources
With print texts, it is easy to identify the authors and their credentials, as well as the publisher and their reputation. With electronic resources like websites, though, it can be trickier to assess the reliability of information. Students should be alert when gathering information from the Internet. Understanding the significance of website **domains**—which include identification strings of a site—can help. Website domains ending in *.edu* are educational sites and tend to offer more reliable research in their field. A *.org* ending tends to be used by nonprofit organizations and other community groups, *.com* indicates a privately-owned website, and a *.gov* site is run by the government. Websites affiliated with official organizations, research groups, or institutes of learning are more likely to offer relevant, fact-checked, and reliable information.

Using Technology

Students in a modern classroom have access to a wide variety of instructional resources. From teacher-led instruction and classroom activities, traditional textbooks, encyclopedias, nonfiction magazines, and customized classroom libraries to desktop computers, iPads, tablets, laptops, online tutorials, and smart boards, there is a plethora of information waiting to be discovered. Learning how to integrate traditional written, visual, and oral information to other information provided on a multimedia platform can prove challenging, but it is well worth the effort. Since the vast majority of children from the primary school years and older are well equipped at using a variety of technology-based resources, educators who integrate technology in the classroom will likely succeed in helping children to progress both academically and socially. The classroom is as much a social setting as it is academic, and as society changes, so must the instructional approaches.

Time management is one of the initial tasks facing educators when setting up their academic year. Educators are responsible for teaching a wide range of subjects, specific domains within each subject, and numerous skills within each domain. Designing long-range plans that take all of this into account and forming a framework for the academic year is the most logical starting point.

From this framework, educators can determine how to teach each discipline with an effective, time-management approach. Taking the number of students, the possible varying academic and social levels, socioeconomic differences, and language barriers into account, teachers can begin to develop differentiated instructional approaches that cater to all the needs in the classroom. It is at this stage that both traditional resources and technology must find a way to complement each other in the classroom.

For instance, one effective approach is to instruct children to ensure that every research project involves a minimum of two textbook sources as well as a minimum of two technology-based sources. When introducing new topics or reinforcing a lesson, educators are still highly encouraged to use visual aids in the classroom, including word walls, personal dictionaries, and classroom labels. Modeling the effective use of hand-held books, reference guides, and magazines also provides children the opportunity to see how valuable written information continues to be in the world of education.

In order for children to experience a well-rounded, quality education, instructional days should be divided between effective, quality instruction, independent exploration and learning, and positive social interaction. Since the needs of children vary in each classroom, as well as their academic and social levels, each educator's decision on how to divide instructional time will also vary. However, having access to technology is paramount in every classroom and at every grade level.

Technology in the classroom helps children to become more actively engaged and encourages independent learning with the use of student-centered, project-based activities. From virtual math tools to collaborative class blogs, there are many ways for students to effectively engage in technology in the classroom.

Although technology plays an important role in the modern classroom, it is still important for educators to guide children, helping them use the technology in an effective, efficient, and responsible manner. Teaching children about cyber-bullying, copyright, plagiarism, and digital footprints will inevitably strengthen their ability to responsibly and safely conduct themselves online.

Educators also use technology for lesson planning, assessments, and evaluation. With a number of online programs available, educators are able to provide students, colleagues, administration, and parents with effective feedback and to develop and evaluate high-quality formative and summative assessments in an efficient manner.

By combining the use of technology along with teacher-centered instruction and traditional textbooks, educators will undoubtedly help to create a classroom with children who are actively engaged throughout the instructional day.

Media Resources

Multimedia presentations, such as PowerPoint or SlideShare, have been traditionally most effective at the higher education levels. However, as young children are more and more exposed to a world of technology, educators at the primary years are beginning to employ multimedia presentations in the classroom.

If carefully planned out, multimedia presentations can be used to enhance comprehension on virtually any subject. Using powerful graphic imagery that is directly relevant to the topic—coupled with effective textual language or audio—has been particularly effective in a growing number of classrooms.

Presenting students with the challenge of creating their own multimedia presentations can also be very rewarding for educators and students alike. Either independently, in pairs, or in groups, children take the learning process into their own hands with the opportunity to demonstrate the knowledge of a given subject by employing relevant written text and graphics.

Practice Questions

1. What contributes the most to schema development?
    a. Reading comprehension
    b. Structural analysis
    c. Written language
    d. Background knowledge

2. Which of the following is NOT an essential component of effective fluency instruction?
    a. Spelling
    b. Feedback
    c. Guidance
    d. Practice

3. The Directed-Reading Think-Aloud (DRTA) method helps students to do what?
    a. Build prior knowledge by exploring audiovisual resources before a reading
    b. Predict what will occur in a text and search the text to verify the predictions
    c. Identify, define, and review unfamiliar terms
    d. Understand the format of multiple types and genres of text

4. A teacher assigns a writing prompt in order to assess her students' reading skills. Which of the following can be said about this form of reading assessment?
    a. It is the most beneficial way to assess reading comprehension
    b. It is invalid because a student's ability to read and write are unrelated
    c. It is erroneous since the strength of a student's reading and writing vocabulary may differ
    d. It is the worst way to assess reading comprehension

5. When does scaffolded reading occur?
    a. A student hears a recording of herself reading a text in order to set personal reading goals.
    b. A student receives assistance and feedback on strategies to utilize while reading from someone else.
    c. A student is given extra time to find the answers to predetermined questions.
    d. A student is pulled out of a class to receive services elsewhere.

6. What are the three interconnected indicators of reading fluency?
    a. Phonetics, word morphology, and listening comprehension
    b. Accuracy, rate, and prosody
    c. Syntax, semantics, and vocabulary
    d. Word exposure, phonetics, and decodable skills

7. Which of the following about effective independent reading is NOT true?
    a. Students should read texts that are below their reading levels during independent reading.
    b. Students need to first demonstrate fluency before reading independently.
    c. Students who don't yet display automaticity should whisper to themselves when reading aloud.
    d. Students who demonstrate automaticity in decoding should be held accountable during independent reading.

8. Timed oral reading can be used to assess which of the following?
    a. Phonics
    b. Listening comprehension
    c. Reading rate
    d. Background knowledge

9. Syntax is best described as what?
    a. The arrangement of words into sentences
    b. The study of language meaning
    c. The study of grammar and language structure
    d. The proper formatting of a written text

10. What do informal reading assessments allow that standardized reading assessments do NOT allow?
    a. The application of grade-level norms towards a student's reading proficiency
    b. The personalization of reading assessments in order to differentiate instruction based on the need(s) of individual students
    c. The avoidance of partialities in the interpretation of reading assessments
    d. The comparison of an individual's reading performance to that of other students in the class

11. When building a class library, a teacher should be cognizant of the importance of what?
    a. Providing fiction that contains concepts relating to the background knowledge of all students in the class.
    b. Utilizing only nonfictional text that correlates to state and national standards in order to reinforce academic concept knowledge.
    c. Utilizing a single genre of text in order to reduce confusion of written structures.
    d. Including a wide range of fiction and nonfiction texts at multiple reading levels.

12. Samantha is in second grade and struggles with fluency. Which of the following strategies is likely to be most effective in improving Samantha's reading fluency?
    a. The teacher prompts Samantha when she pauses upon coming across an unknown word when reading aloud.
    b. The teacher records Samantha as she reads aloud.
    c. The teacher reads a passage out loud several times to Samantha and then has Samantha read the same passage.
    d. The teacher uses read-alouds and verbalizes contextual strategies that can be used to identify unfamiliar words.

13. Reading fluency is best described as the ability to do what?
    a. Read smoothly and accurately
    b. Comprehend what is read
    c. Demonstrate phonetic awareness
    d. Properly pronounce a list of words

14. Poems are often an effective device when teaching what skill?
    a. Fluency
    b. Spelling
    c. Writing
    d. Word decoding

15. A teacher needs to assess students' accuracy in reading grade-appropriate, high frequency, and irregular sight words. Which of the following strategies would be most appropriate for this purpose?

    a. The teacher gives students a list of words to study for a spelling test that will be administered the following week.

    b. The teacher allows each student to bring their favorite book from home and has each student read their selected text aloud independently.

    c. The teacher administers the Stanford Structural Analysis assessment to determine students' rote memory and application of morphemes contained within the words.

    d. The teacher records how many words each student reads correctly when reading aloud a list of a teacher-selected, grade-appropriate words.

16 What type of text(s) should be included when teaching reading comprehension in the classroom?

    a. Expository/informational

    b. Nonfiction and fiction

    c. Only nonfiction

    d. Basal readers

17. What is a summative assessment?

    a. A formal assessment that is given at the end of a unit of study

    b. An informal assessment that is given at the end of a unit of study

    c. An assessment that is given daily and is usually only a few questions in length, based on the day's objective

    d. An assessment given at the end of the week that is usually based on observation

18. How are typographic features useful when teaching reading comprehension?

    a. Typographic features are graphics used to illustrate the story and help students visualize the text.

    b. Typographic features give the answers in boldfaced print.

    c. Typographic features are not helpful when teaching reading comprehension and should not be used.

    d. Typographic features are print in boldface, italics, and subheadings, used to display changes in topics or to highlight important vocabulary or content.

19. What do English Language Learners need to identify prior to comprehending text?

    a. Vocabulary

    b. Figurative language

    c. Author's purpose

    d. Setting

20. What kind of assessment is most beneficial for students with special needs?

    a. Frequent and ongoing

    b. Weekly

    c. Monthly

    d. Summative assessments only at the end of a unit of study

21. Which is NOT a reason that independent reading is important for developing reading comprehension?
    a. To develop a lifelong love of reading
    b. To encourage students to read a genre they enjoy
    c. So that students can read at their own pace
    d. To visit the reading corner, which is an area of the classroom that is restful and enjoyable

22. Why are purposeful read alouds by a teacher important to enhance reading comprehension?
    a. They encourage students to unwind from a long day and reading lesson.
    b. They encourage students to listen for emphasis and voice.
    c. They encourage students to compare the author's purpose versus the teacher's objective.
    d. They encourage students to work on important work from earlier in the day while listening to a story.

23. Which of the following is the definition of *syntax*?
    a. The meaning of words
    b. The order of words in a sentence
    c. The grouping of large complex words
    d. Highlighted, or boldfaced words

24. What is "text evidence" when referring to answering a comprehension question?
    a. Taking phrases directly from the text itself to answer a question
    b. Using a variety of resources to find the answer
    c. Using technology and websites to locate an answer
    d. Paraphrasing and using a student's own words to answer the question

25. What allows readers to effectively translate print into recognizable speech?
    a. Fluency
    b. Spelling
    c. Phonics
    d. Word decoding

26. Which of the following is the MOST important reason why group-based discussions in the classroom enhance reading comprehension?
    a. They promote student discussions without the teacher present.
    b. They promote student discussions with a friend.
    c. They promote student discussions so that those who didn't understand the text can get answers from another student.
    d. They give all students a voice and allow them to share their answer, rather than one student sharing an answer with the class

27. Which of the following skills is NOT useful when initially helping students understand and comprehend a piece of text?
    a. Graphic organizers
    b. Note-taking
    c. Small intervention groups
    d. Extension projects and papers

28. Why are intervention groups important to advanced learners?
    a. They are not useful, as they do not need intervention in a particular skill
    b. They can be used to teach struggling students
    c. They can be given more advanced and complex work
    d. They can be given tasks to do in the classroom while others are meeting for intervention

29. Which of the following can be useful when working with intervention groups of struggling readers?
    a. Having the teacher read aloud a text to the students while they take notes
    b. Having students read the text silently
    c. Giving independent work and explaining the directions in detail before they take it back to their seat
    d. Providing games for them to play while the teacher observes

30. What should be taught and mastered first when teaching reading comprehension?
    a. Theme
    b. Word analysis and fluency
    c. Text evidence
    d. Writing

31. What is the method called that teachers use before and after reading to improve critical thinking and comprehension?
    a. Self-monitoring comprehension
    b. KWL charts
    c. Metacognitive skills
    d. Directed reading-thinking activities

32. When a student looks back at a previous reading section for information, he or she is using which of the following?
    a. Self-monitoring comprehension
    b. KWL charts
    c. Metacognitive skills
    d. Directed reading-thinking activities

33. Which choice of skills is NOT part of Bloom's Taxonomy?
    a. Remembering and understanding
    b. Applying and analyzing
    c. Listening and speaking
    d. Evaluating and creating

34. What is the spelling stage of a student who looks at a word and is able to tell the teacher that the letters spell C-A-T, but the who cannot actually say the word?
    a. Alphabetic Spelling
    b. Within Word Pattern Spelling
    c. Derivational Relations Spelling
    d. Emergent Spelling

35. Predicting, Summarizing, Questioning, and Clarifying are steps of what?
   a. Reciprocal teaching
   b. Comprehensive teaching
   c. Activation teaching
   d. Summative teaching

36. When a student asks, "What do I know?", "What do I want to know?", and "What have I learned?" and records the answers in a table, he or she is using which of the following?
   a. Self-monitoring comprehension
   b. KWL charts
   c. Metacognitive skills
   d. Directed reading-thinking activities

37. What technique might an author use to let the reader know that the main character was in a car crash as a child?
   a. Point of view
   b. Characterization
   c. Figurative language
   d. Flashback

38. A graphic organizer is a method of achieving what?
   a. Integrating knowledge and ideas
   b. Generating questions
   c. Determining point of view
   d. Determining the author's purpose

39. A student is trying to decide if a character is telling the truth about having stolen candy. After the student reads that the character is playing with an empty candy wrapper in her pocket, the student decides the character is guilty. This is an example of what?
   a. Flashback
   b. Making inferences
   c. Style
   d. Figurative language

40. What is the method of categorizing text by its structure and literary elements called?
   a. Fiction
   b. Nonfiction
   c. Genre
   d. Plot

41. A reader is distracted from following a story because he's having trouble understanding why a character has decided to cut school, so the reader jumps to the next page to find out where the character is headed. This is an example of what?
   a. Self-monitoring comprehension
   b. KWL charts
   c. Metacognitive skills
   d. Directed reading-thinking activities

42. Phonemic Awareness, Phonics, Fluency, Vocabulary, and Comprehension are the five basic elements of what?

    a. Bloom's Taxonomy

    b. Spelling instruction

    c. Reading education

    d. Genre

43. A child reads the story *Little Red Riding Hood* aloud. He easily pronounces the words, uses an apprehensive tone to show that the main character should not be leaving the path, adds a scary voice for the Big Bad Wolf, and reads the story at a pace that engages the class. What are these promising signs of?

    a. Reading fluency

    b. Phonemic awareness

    c. Reading comprehension

    d. Working memory

44. A student is trying to read the word "preferred." She first recognizes the word "red" at the end, then sounds out the rest of the word by breaking it down into "pre," then "fer," then "red." Finally she puts it together and says "preferred." This student is displaying what attribute?

    a. Phonemic awareness

    b. Phonics

    c. Fluency

    d. Vocabulary

45. A class silently reads a passage on the American Revolution. Once they are done, the teacher asks who were the two sides fighting, why were they fighting, and who won. What skill is the teacher gauging?

    a. Orthographic development

    b. Fluency

    c. Comprehension

    d. Phonics

Answer Explanations

1. D: A schema is a framework or structure that stores and retrieves multiple, interrelated learning elements as a single packet of knowledge. Children who have greater exposure to life events have greater schemas. Thus, students who bring extensive background knowledge to the classroom are likely to experience easier automation when reading. In this way, background knowledge and reading comprehension are directly related. Likewise, students who have greater background knowledge are able to learn a greater number of new concepts at a faster rate.

2. A: Practice is an essential component of effective fluency instruction. When teachers provide daily opportunities for students to learn words and utilize word-analysis skills, accuracy and rate will likely increase. Oral reading accompanied by guidance and feedback from teachers, peers, or parents has a significant positive impact on fluency. In order to be beneficial, such feedback needs to target specific areas in which students need improvement, as well as strategies that students can use in order to improve their areas of need. Such feedback increases students' awareness so that they can independently make needed modifications to improve fluency.

3. B: DRTA, or Directed Reading-Thinking Activity, incorporates both read-alouds and think-alouds. During a DRTA, students make predictions about what they will read in order to set a purpose for reading, give cognitive focus, and activate prior knowledge. Students use reading comprehension in order to verify their predictions.

4. C: There are five types of vocabulary: listening, speaking, written, sight, and meaning. Most often, listening vocabulary contains the greatest number of words. This is usually followed by speaking vocabulary, sight reading vocabulary, meaning vocabulary, and written vocabulary. Formal written language usually utilizes a richer vocabulary than everyday oral language. Thus, students show differing strengths in reading vocabulary and writing vocabulary. Likewise, a student's reading ability will most likely differ when assessed via a reading assessment versus a writing sample.

5. B: Scaffolded opportunities occur when a teacher helps students by giving them support, offering immediate feedback, and suggesting strategies. In order to be beneficial, such feedback needs to help students identify areas that need improvement. Much like oral reading feedback, this advice increases students' awareness so they can independently make needed modifications in order to improve fluency.

Scaffolding is lessened as the student becomes a more independent reader. Struggling readers, students with reading difficulties or disabilities, and students with special needs especially benefit from direct instruction and feedback that teaches decoding and analysis of unknown words, automaticity in key sight words, and correct expression and phrasing.

6. B: Key indicators of reading fluency include accuracy, rate, and prosody. Phonetics and decodable skills aid fluency. Syntax, semantics, word morphology, listening comprehension, and word exposure aid vocabulary development.

7. A: Once students become fluent readers, independent reading can begin. Students who don't yet display automaticity may need to read out loud or whisper to themselves during independent reading time. Independent silent reading accompanied by comprehension accountability is an appropriate strategy for students who demonstrate automaticity in their decoding skills. Also, each student should be provided with a text that matches his or her reading level.

8. C: The most common measurement of reading rate includes the oral contextual timed readings of students. During a timed reading, the number of errors made within a given amount of time is recorded. This data can be used to identify if a student's rate is improving and if the rate falls within the recommended fluency rates for their grade level.

9. A: Syntax refers to the arrangement of words and phrases to form well-developed sentences and paragraphs. Semantics has to do with language meaning. Grammar is a composite of all systems and structures utilized within a language and includes syntax, word morphology, semantics, and phonology. Cohesion and coherence of oral and written language are promoted through a full understanding of syntax, semantics, and grammar.

10. B: Informal reading assessments allow teachers to create differentiated assessments that target reading skills of individual students. In this way, teachers can gain insight into a student's reading strengths and weaknesses. Informal assessments can help teachers decide what content and strategies need to be targeted. However, standardized reading assessments provide all students with the same structure to assess multiple skills at one time. Standardized reading assessments cannot be individualized. Such assessments are best used for gaining an overview of student reading abilities.

11. D: Students within a single classroom come with various background knowledge, interests, and needs. Thus, it's unrealistic to find texts that apply to all. Students benefit when a wide range of fiction and nonfiction texts are available in a variety of genres, promoting differentiated instruction.

12. D: This answer alludes to both read-alouds and think-alouds. Modeling of fluency can be done through read-alouds. Proper pace, phrasing, and expression of text can be modeled when teachers read aloud to their students. During think-alouds, teachers verbalize their thought processes when orally reading a selection. The teacher's explanations may describe strategies they use as they read to monitor their comprehension. In this way, teachers explicitly model the metacognition processes that good readers use to construct meaning from a text.

13. A: Reading fluency is the ability to accurately read at a socially acceptable pace and with proper expression. Phonetic awareness leads to the proper pronunciation of words and fluency. Once students are able to read fluently, concentration is no longer dedicated toward the process of reading. Instead, students can concentrate on the meaning of a text. Thus, in the developmental process of reading, comprehension follows fluency.

14. A: Poems are an effective method for teaching fluency, since rhythmic sounds and rhyming words build a child's understanding of phonemic awareness.

15. D: Accuracy is measured via the percentage of words that are read correctly with in a given text. Word-reading accuracy is often measured by counting the number of errors that occur per 100 words of oral reading. This information is used to select the appropriate level of text for an individual.

16. B: Nonfiction and fiction texts should both be used. This could encompass the Choices A, C, and D, which include expository, informational, nonfiction, and use of the school's basal reader, but should not be limited to just one of these. Utilizing many different types of text and genres when teaching reading comprehension is key to success.

17. A: Summative assessments are formal assessments that are given at the end of a unit of study. These assessments are usually longer in length. They are not completed daily. These summative assessments shouldn't be confused with informal assessments, which are used more frequently to determine mastery of the day's objective. However, summative assessments may be used to determine students' mastery, in order to form intervention groups thereafter.

18. D: Typographic features are important when teaching reading comprehension as the boldfaced, highlighted, or italics notify a student when a new vocabulary word or idea is present. Subtitles and headings can also alert a student to a change in topic or idea. These features are also important when answering questions, as a student may be able to easily find the answer with these typographic features present.

19. A: English Language Learners should master vocabulary and word usages in order to fully comprehend text. Figurative language, an author's purpose, and settings are more complex areas and are difficult for English Language Learners. These areas can be addressed once ELL students understand the meaning of words. In order to master comprehension skills, vocabulary and the English language need to be mastered first, but comprehension can still be difficult. Figurative language is culture-based, and inferences may be difficult for those with a different cultural background.

20. A: Assessments should always be frequent and ongoing for all students, but especially for those with special needs. These assessments may be informal, but given daily after direct instruction and modeling. Summative assessments are important, but this should not be the first and only assessment during a unit of study, as these types of assessments are given at the end of a unit of study. Weekly and monthly assessments are not frequent enough for instructors to identify struggling areas and for successful remediation and intervention.

21. D: Although the reading corner should be a restful and enjoyable place to encourage students to read independently, it does not enhance reading comprehension directly. Choices A, B, and C all encourage enhancement of reading comprehension. Giving students a chance to read independently allows them to choose books they enjoy, read at their own pace, and develop a lifelong enjoyment of reading.

22. B: Purposeful teacher read alouds allow students to listen to a story for voice emphasis and tone. This will help students when they are reading independently as well. Although students may find this time restful or a chance to catch up on old work, neither is the main purpose. Students may use this time to take notes on the reading, but students should only be listening to the story being read and not doing other work.

23. B: Syntax is the order of words in a sentence. The order of words in a sentence is important to meaning, but Choice A is not the direct definition of syntax. Choice C is incorrect because syntax does not mean grouping of complex words. Choice D is incorrect because highlighted and boldfaced words refer to typographic features in a text, not to syntax.

24. A: "Text evidence" refers to taking phrases and sentences directly from the text and writing them in the answer. Students are not asked to paraphrase, nor use any other resources to address the answer. Therefore, Choices B, C, and D are incorrect.

25. C: Phonics allows readers to effectively translate print into recognizable speech. It essentially enables young readers to translate printed words into recognizable speech. If children lack proficiency in phonics, their ability to read fluently and to increase vocabulary will be limited.

26. D: Text-based discussions, like think-pair-share, encourage all students to speak rather than having just one student share an answer. Each student is given time to collaborate with another student and share their thoughts. It is not intended for one student to give another student the answers, which is why Choice C is incorrect. Although Choices A and B might be correct, they are not the MOST important reason that text-based discussions are useful in the classroom.

27. D: Extension projects and papers should be used to challenge advanced learners, not learners developing comprehension skills. Graphic organizers, taking notes, and small intervention groups can aid reading comprehension. Graphic organizers and taking notes are great ways for a student to outline key parts of the text. Small intervention groups set up by the instructor can then focus on individual needs.

28. C: Advanced students can benefit from intervention groups by allowing the students to be challenged with more complex assignments. These assignments can be worked on independently and can include more difficult questions or higher level vocabulary. Even short projects may be beneficial for these advanced students to work on throughout the week.

29. A: Small intervention groups can benefit from a teacher reading a text or small book aloud while students listen and take notes. This helps struggling students to focus on reading comprehension rather than having to decode words. Intervention time is not meant for a teacher to give independent work nor to just provide observation without support.

30. B: Word analysis and fluency should be mastered before teaching theme, text evidence, and writing. For English Language Learners and struggling readers, word analysis and fluency are often difficult barriers, which is why comprehension skills are not initially mastered. Theme is often a complex and inferential skill, which is developed later on. Text evidence is pulling answers to comprehension questions directly from a text and cannot be accomplished until readers can fluently read and understand the text. Writing skills generally come after comprehension skills are underway.

31. D: Teachers use directed reading-thinking activities before and after reading to improve critical thinking and reading comprehension. Metacognitive skills are when learners think about their thinking. Self-monitoring is when children are asked to think as they read and ask themselves if what they have just read makes sense. KWL charts help guide students to identify what they already know about a given topic.

32. C: Asking oneself a comprehension question is a metacognition skill. Readers with metacognitive skills have learned to think about thinking. It gives students control over their learning while they read. KWL charts help students to identify what they already know about a given topic.

33. C: Listening and speaking are not part of Bloom's Taxonomy. The six parts are remembering, understanding, applying, analyzing, evaluating, and creating.

34. D: During the Emergent Spelling stage, children can identify letters but not the corresponding sounds. The other choices are all fictitious.

35. A: Reciprocal teaching involves predicting, summarizing, questioning, and clarifying. The other choices are all fictitious.

36. B: KWL charts are an effective method of activating prior knowledge and taking advantage of students' curiosity. Students can create a KWL (*Know/Want to know/Learned*) chart to prepare for any unit of instruction and to generate questions about a topic.

37. D: Flashback is a technique used to give more background information in a story. None of the other concepts are directly related to going back in time.

38. A: Graphic organizers are a method of integrating knowledge and ideas. A graphic organizer can be one of many different visual tools for connecting concepts to help students understand information.

39. B: Making inferences is a method of deriving meaning in writing that is intended by the author but not explicitly stated. A flashback is a scene set earlier than the main story. Style is a general term for the way something is done. Figurative language is text that is not to be taken literally.

40. C: Genre is a means of categorizing text by its structure and literary elements. Fiction and nonfiction are both genre categories. Plot is the sequence of events that make a story happen.

41. A: Scanning future portions of the text for information that helps resolve a question is an example of self-monitoring. Self-monitoring takes advantage students' natural ability to recognize when they understand the reading and when they do not. KWL charts are used to help guide students to identify what they already know about a given topic. Metacognitive skills are when learners think about their thinking. Directed reading-thinking activities are done before and after reading to improve critical thinking and reading comprehension skills.

42. C: The five basic components of reading education are phonemic awareness, phonics, fluency, vocabulary, and comprehension.

43. A: If a child can accurately read text with consistent speed and appropriate expression while demonstrating comprehension, the child is said to have reading fluency skills. Without the ability to read fluently, a child's reading comprehension (Choice C) will be limited.

44. B: Phonics is the ability to apply letter-sound relationships and letter patterns in order to accurately pronounce written words. Phonemic awareness is the understanding that words are comprised of a combination of sounds. Fluency is an automatic recognition and accurate interpretation of text. Vocabulary is the body of words that a person knows.

45. C: Comprehension is the level of content understanding that a student demonstrates after reading. Orthographic development is a cumulative process for learning to read, with each skill building on the previously mastered skill. Fluency is an automatic recognition and accurate interpretation of text. Phonics is the ability to apply letter-sound relationships and letter patterns in order to accurately pronounce written words.

Leadership Skills and Specialized Knowledge of Pedagogical Principles and Instructional Practices

Reading Specialist Skills

Diagnosing Reading Difficulties

There are many factors that influence a child's language acquisition. A child's physical age, level of maturity, home and school experiences, general attitudes toward learning, and home languages are just some of the many influences on a child's literacy development. However, a child's **language acquisition** progresses through the following generalized stages:

Stage	Examples	Typical Age
Preproduction	does not verbalize/ nods yes and no	zero to six months
Early production	one to two word responses	six to twelve months
Speech emergence	produces simple sentences	one to three years
Intermediate fluency	simple to more complex sentences	three to five years
Advanced fluency	near native level of speech	five to seven years

While this applies to language acquisition in one's home language, the very same stages apply to English language learners (ELLs). Since effective communication in any given language requires much more than a mere collection of vocabulary words that one can accurately translate, paying particular attention to each stage in language acquisition is imperative. In addition to vocabulary knowledge, language acquisition involves the study and gradual mastery of intonation, a language's dialects—if applicable—and the various nuances in a language regarding word use, expression, and cultural contexts. With time, effort, patience, and effective instructional approaches, both students and educators will begin to see progress in language acquisition.

Second language acquisition does not happen overnight. When educators take the time to study each stage and implement a variety of effective instructional approaches, progress and transition from one stage to the next will undoubtedly be less cumbersome and more consistent. In the early stages of language acquisition, children are often silently observing their new language environment. At these early stages, listening comprehension should be emphasized with the use of read alouds, music, and visual aids. Educators should be mindful of their vocabulary usage by consciously choosing to speak slowly and to use shorter, less complex vocabulary. Modeling during these beginning stages is also very effective. If the educator has instructed the class to open a book for instance, they can open a book as a visual guide. If it is time to line up, the educator can verbally state the instruction and then walk to the door to begin the line.

During the **pre-production stage**, educators and classmates may assist ELLs by restating words or sentences that were uttered incorrectly, instead of pointing out errors. When modeling the correct language usage instead of pointing out errors, ELL learners may be less intimidated to practice their new language.

As students progress into the **early production stage**, they will benefit from exercises that challenge them to produce simple words and sentences with the assistance of visual cues. The educator should ask students to point to various pictures or symbols and produce words or sentences to describe the images they see. At the early production and **speech emergent stages**, ELL students are now ready to answer more diverse questions as they begin to develop a more complex vocabulary. Working in heterogeneous pairs and small groups with native speakers will help ELL students develop a more advanced vocabulary.

At the beginning and **intermediate fluency stages**, ELLs may be asked questions that require more advanced cognitive skills. Asking for opinions on a certain subject or requiring students to brainstorm and find ways to explain a given phenomenon are other ways to strengthen language proficiency and increase vocabulary.

When a child reaches the **advanced fluency stage**, he or she will be confident in social and academic language environments. This is an opportune time to introduce and/or increase his or her awareness of idiomatic expressions and language nuances.

World-Class Instructional Design and Assessment (WIDA) is a consortium of various departments of education throughout the United States that design and implement proficiency standards and assessments for English language learners and Spanish language learners. Primarily focusing on listening, speaking, reading, and writing, WIDA has designed and implemented English language development standards and offers professional development for educators, as well as educational research on instructional best practices. The five English language proficiency standards according to WIDA are as follows:

English Language Proficiency Standards—WIDA

1. Within a school environment, ELL students require communication skills for both social and instructional purposes.

2. Effective communication involving information, ideas, and concepts are necessary for ELL students to be academically successful in the area of Language Arts.

3. Effective communication involving information, ideas, and concepts are necessary for ELL students to be academically successful in the area of Mathematics.

4. Effective communication involving information, ideas, and concepts are necessary for ELL students to be academically successful in the area of Science.

5. Effective communication involving information, ideas, and concepts are necessary for ELL students to be academically successful in the area of Social Studies.

According to WIDA, mastering the understanding, interpretation, and application of the four **language domains**—listening, speaking, reading, and writing—is essential for language proficiency. Listening requires ELL students to be able to process, understand, interpret, and evaluate spoken language. Speaking proficiently allows ELL students to communicate their thoughts, opinions, and desires orally in a variety of situations and for a variety of audiences. The ability to read fluently involves the processing, understanding, interpreting, and evaluating of written language with a high level of accuracy, and writing proficiency allows ELL students to engage actively in written communication across a multitude of disciplines and for a variety of purposes.

Since language acquisition involves the ELL students, their families, their classmates, educators, principals and administrators, as well as test and curriculum developers, WIDA strives to ensure that the English Language Proficiency Standards reflect both the social and academic areas of language development.

Types of Disabilities for Literacy Development

When students display intense or specific learning difficulties with reading material, it may be indicative that they have learning disabilities. It's important for educators to understand that learning disabilities are relatively common and can be overcome. To help students do this, however, an instructor must be mindful of the types and effects of various learning disorders. Addressing these learning disabilities is crucial for early development.

Reading disorders, as they sound, are when students exhibit difficulties reading or understanding the written word. One of the most common reading disorders is **dyslexia**. A common sign of dyslexia is that the student will reverse the order of letters and thus confuse sounds or misread words. This disorder isn't a lapse in intelligence at all; many individuals can speak just fine and understand the words and principles. However, visually, they have trouble interpreting the writing. Specialized instruction focuses on giving students methods for reading text more carefully to identify what's written.

Another type of learning disorder category deals with difficulties students face when physically writing content. Students with this type of disorder may read passages without any problems, but when it comes to spelling out words and constructing sentences, there are recurring issues. This difficulty with written expression is called **dysgraphia**, which is characterized by poor handwriting and constant grammatical and spelling errors. While this may seem common in early learners, students with dysgraphia can display these issues at older age ranges. Another core aspect of dysgraphia is that students have difficulties expressing themselves in writing. While they have good ideas, they may have trouble presenting them in a logical sequence. Naturally, the instructor will want to customize the instruction for these students, focusing on writing and composition exercises to address the problem areas and help students regain confidence in their abilities.

It's important to note that disorders cannot be cured the way a doctor might treat an infection. Differentiated instruction can help address some of the core issues of learning disabilities while also boosting student morale. This process will be expedited by keeping students engaged and encouraging them throughout the process; these factors will determine how hard students strive to learn and overcome issues.

High-Achieving Students

Classes will usually have high-achieving students who seem to be way beyond the levels of the majority of the class. In addition to addressing students who struggle with reading, it's important to challenge students who are more advanced in their abilities. This serves to both engage these students and keep them attentive in class to avoid disruptions. Additionally, this approach will help students accelerate their education and reach their potential. To address all levels of students, it's important for an instructor to be flexible with their lessons and adaptable to change.

When designing instruction, specialists should consider how challenging material should be presented. The **zone of proximal development** looks at what students are capable of doing without assistance and what they need help with; essentially, this is the margin of capability. Each student has their own zone, so being able to gauge where the class generally stands can help teachers define lesson parameters and expectations within an individual's zone. If students are struggling, the instruction can be less challenging and adjusted as improvements are made. This can be done by using easier reading texts and slower, more dedicated lessons or learning activities. Alternatively, this methodology can be used to adjust instruction for high-achieving readers by reversing this process.

When students have advanced reading skills, their proximal development zone will be greater than the lower level of readers; they'll be more independent and ready to take on tougher material. One way to challenge these students is to assign them harder reading texts or let them choose from advanced reading selections. Instructors should still monitor the accuracy of their work, but these students will require less focus on basic reading principles. With more advanced instruction, performance expectations should be raised to make sure students are still meeting core learning objectives.

Class or group activities can also be tailored to suit all levels of reading ability. Reading and response or free-writing activities will let students explore their own abilities while not being restricted by specific guidelines. Allowing students to create an alternate ending to a story, present a response, or create independent reading projects allows them to use their skills in a way in which they're comfortable.

Theories of Personality and Learning Behaviors

Psychology influences how individuals think, process information, and interact with others. In addition to inherent thought processes, psychology also looks at external influences that make people think or act certain ways. As a reading instructor, understanding general psychology and personality traits is important because it will help indicate student needs or disconnects with the material. If a student has behavioral issues or seems unusually anxious, there are probably hidden reasons behind this. This knowledge will help the instructor better relate to the student and address the student if issues arise.

Concrete thinking, the simple act of knowing and understanding what can be seen or experienced, occurs very early in development. This begins with the formation of the perspective; children encounter things and then form views about them, just like they do when they read material or listen to spoken words. This reflects how people immediately understand the world. From this, the next stage in psychological development involves the use of symbols; students can symbolize what they know or how they understand it. This is why drawing and imagery are such powerful tools in early development; children can project their ideas and understanding onto the page through physical representation. When reading information, the mind processes and interprets it. Often, a student's initial understanding of the material is subconsciously related to symbols and meanings previously encountered. This would explain why a child may have a different opinion on a subject or why they interpret the reading differently.

95

Around ages seven or eight, children develop what's known as the **theory of mind**. This means they are able to acknowledge and relate to several points of view besides their own. While this marks a broadening of perspective, it can also result in confusion and difficulty with the subject matter. Comprehension sets in when students can balance their individual opinions while clearly understanding the intended contextual meaning.

Memory is another important psychological factor. Memory influences perspective and enables people to interpret and learn new information. Sometimes learning issues stem from problems with memory. This can include difficulty recalling information or being unable to learn correct information quickly.

Influence of Cultural Contexts

Recall that language evolves and develops over time. While there may be a standard version of a given language, inevitably, the language will undertake alterations in use and pronunciation based on cultural interactions. Various cultures speak differently, so separate areas or subcultures of a given country will develop their own idiomatic phrases of the given language. Accents will be altered over time, which also differentiates the pronunciation of various words. Again, these cultural influences are not incorrect or bad representations of the English language. Being respectful of all these cultures and cultural influences is very important. Other cultures or accents aren't wrong; the instructor is merely teaching Standard American English to students.

Accents may be apparent in the classroom, which may make certain words sound unfamiliar or alter the individual student's pronunciation. Accent and general cultural influences can also affect how students think words and phrases should sound. It's important not to admonish children for this but instead to provide feedback on correct pronunciation. There are several types of accents in the United States alone, including the northern, southern, and midwestern accents of American English speakers. An instructor may notice stronger vowels and alternate wording influenced by these regional accents and dialects. Foreign students or students learning English as a second language may carry an accent from their original language as well. Recall that cultural values and experiences may also alter how a student reads and interprets English content. Therefore, discussing the reading is always a good practice to ensure everyone is on the same page.

Vocabulary choices may also differ among students based on their upbringing. For example, regional dialects tend to favor some terms more than others. Sometimes this will entail the use of alternate grammatical forms. For example, *ain't* is used in parts of the South to replace *is not* or *isn't*. One of the reasons vocabulary is emphasized in literacy development is to ensure that students learn a broad range of words besides terms with which they may already be familiar. A good vocabulary will also give students an effective means to express themselves, both orally and in writing.

Educational Measurement and Evaluation

Being able to effectively evaluate student performance enables teachers to develop the best instructions to help their students reach their potential. Reading assessments are key to identifying individual strengths and weaknesses, so both formal and informal assessments should be used in the classroom. Being able to successfully gauge individual reading levels means looking at essential performance indicators of rate and accuracy.

An **oral fluency assessment** should be used to see how students approach reading as a whole. This assessment examines the number of words the student can read within one minute. A text relative to the student's level should be used. For beginning learners, the difficulty of the text can be below their initial level too. Based on how many correct words the student reads, an instructor can determine how advanced they are in developing reading skills. The number of times students incorrectly read words and the length of time it takes for them to read the text will also determine their level of fluency. Fluency assessments also consider the way in which a student reads, whether the language flows or is stalled.

There are four levels of fluency. Levels 1 and 2 reflect nonfluency; these students will need more instruction to hone their reading skills, which may entail various kinds of differentiated instruction. Level 1 is the lowest; these students read word by word and lack tone in their reading. Levels 3 and 4 represent fluent readership. Level 4 reflects the students' ability to read phrases consistently and accurately without having to repeat words. Multiple errors in the reading as well as repetitions may also occur.

When considering the results of such assessments, it's important for instructors to be observant and note where in the reading students struggled and, in addition, to analyze why the reading issues exist. Did certain words confuse the student, or did the student just seem uncertain of their own abilities? Did certain grammatical phrasing confuse the reader? Asking questions like these will help find root problems and enable the specialist to construct actionable plans to steer improvement. It's important to remember that such issues can indicate learning disabilities, so identifying all these issues early is very important. These assessments should also be used to track student progress and assess how effective instruction is in overcoming core issues.

Current Research in Literacy Instruction

It's important for instructors to be cognizant of current research and education trends in order to provide students with the best instruction possible. In 2000, the National Reading Panel published research that indicated the core basis of literary instruction should focus on phonics, phonics awareness, vocabulary, fluency, and comprehension. Instruction in these concentrations can also be tailored to help individual students at varying stages of development.

Phonics focuses on the basic connection between written letters and the sounds they make—the foundation of language. Rhyming exercises have been identified as a major asset in teaching students the relationship between letters and their audible sounds; this will also come into play when full words are constructed. Phonics activities will help build letter and then word familiarity, giving students a firm base for writing interpretation.

Phonemic awareness exercises focus on the way spoken words sound and the way letters interact together to form words. It's important for new readers to be able to deconstruct words into sound sections to build familiarity with how English sounds. One great practice for students is to physically clap out the sound to the words. This gets them used to how syllables come into play within a word and helps students isolate the different sounds in a word. When they can break apart the word sounds, learning to put them together is easier. This method will also help students learn new words.

Incorporating more vocabulary into lessons gives students more terms to work with as well as additional ways to understand written content. There are several proven methods for introducing vocabulary terms. One of the most common practices is pairing new words with images, creating a visual association. Another great exercise is to match the vocabulary terms with their written definitions, establishing the meaning clearly and building memory.

Fluency measures how efficiently and fluidly students can speak the language. This is very important for everyday communication, so exercises such as reading practice are very important. Practices can be timed to assess the rate of reading as well. This will also indicate growing skill level and help pinpoint reading issues.

Comprehension exercises focus on understanding written content, which is vital to interpreting information and drawing conclusions. Reading discussions are key to allowing students to talk about what they've read and explore the ideas presented. Having students summarize what they read will also demonstrate their understanding of the material; this method also makes them practice speaking and critical-thinking skills. Writing reports and answering written questions can also be used.

Leadership Roles of the Reading Specialist

Strategies for Planning, Organizing, Coordinating, and Supervising the Reading Program

When developing a reading lesson, it is important to demonstrate knowledge of standards in reading instruction. All standards-based programs focus on the educator's ability to interpret and instruct the scope of a text while applying state standards. When creating a lesson, a teacher needs to ensure that his or her instruction aligns with the use of their state's adopted materials for instruction and intervention.

To demonstrate the mastery of reading, students should convey their understanding of a text through a written assignment or oral presentation. In order to master the art of writing and presenting, a student needs a complete understanding of the English language and a well-developed vocabulary. Therefore, ELA standards are integrated across the curriculum with reading, writing, speaking, and language skills. These skills are intertwined throughout lessons in order to create a vigorous learning approach. Mastery of this combination of skills demonstrates strong content knowledge and reading comprehension.

Teachers should use a variety of approaches and strategies to impart knowledge to students. Since students have a variety of learning styles, many approaches should be utilized in the classroom. Students need explicit instruction and modeling by the teacher in order to learn a new skill. Instruction also should provide opportunities for students to demonstrate what they have learned and for them to practice independently.

Students should become career and college ready. In order to do so, students should read a variety of literary and informational texts. Such texts may include pieces extending across a wide variety of genres, timelines, and cultural works. Texts are to be complex and should elicit higher-level thinking skills. For example, literature may include Shakespeare. Similarly, informational text may include the founding documents from the United States.

In alignment with the anchor standards for reading, instructors should ensure that students read closely to determine the meaning of a text. Students should make logical inferences and cite specific evidence when speaking or writing in order to support their conclusions. Students should summarize using key details from the text and analyze why and how authors develop ideas throughout the text. Students should learn how to interpret figurative meanings and analyze how specific phrases and paragraphs relate to each other. They also should assess the point of view and purpose of a text. Oral and written evaluation of similarities and differences amongst a variety of formats is important.

In order to achieve the above skills, students should read and comprehend complex literary and informational text with proficiency. Reading, writing, speaking, listening, and language are skills that are to be interwoven within reading instruction so that students master both written and spoken language.

Students should demonstrate the mastery of such skills through written responses to a text that include supporting evidence(s) and citation(s) from the text itself. In addition to writing, students need to perform public speaking projects in order to demonstrate what they have learned from the text.

In addition to intertwining several skills, lessons should include a variety of texts. In kindergarten, literature and informational text should be balanced. Many state standards for reading indicate that from kindergarten through fifth grade, literary and nonfiction text should reflect a 50/50 balance, but educators should check with their own state to make sure. Science and social study texts help to build a rich foundation for informational texts. Basal readers are a good source for fiction and nonfiction text. Building a classroom library can provide a variety of both types of texts. In the primary grades, a classroom library can be a primary source of literary text in order to build an interest in reading. Picture books are also a great way to introduce literary text to early readers.

As students approach fifth grade, informational text found in nonfiction novels and basal readers should become more available. From sixth grade to twelfth grade, greater attention is placed on informational texts. Informational texts should make up 55 percent of a curriculum by the eighth grade and approximately 70 percent of works by the twelfth grade. This is the recommended grade-level distribution of literary and informational passages suggested by the 2009 National Assessment of Educational Progress (NAEP) reading framework.

Teachers will want to include research-based writing lessons of informative, explanatory, and narrative texts. During such lessons, students gather information from multiple sources. Students can use digital media in order to perform such research. This research is used to support claims made in their written responses. Students should address an intended audience in their written work. Additionally, student writing should reflect organization and purpose. Proper citation of the research used within student written responses and technology used to publish work is also important. Published work requires the use of word programs, keyboarding skills, an Internet search engine, and programs such as PowerPoint®, Excel®, or Google docs.

As for the assessment of speaking and listening, instructors should prepare students to engage in conversation effectively individually or in different-sized groups. Students and instructors may use such discussions as informative assessments to judge students' knowledge of a text. Formative evaluations of students' reading ought to include oral presentations as well. Claims made in such student evaluations should be supported with research-based evidence(s) or citations located within the text being discussed.

Students and teachers may use digital media during presentations or assessments in order to allow for more engagement and audience participation. The technology available in the classroom for presentations given by students or teachers may include projectors and Smart Boards. Many touch-screen boards have replaced chalkboards and whiteboards. These computer-based boards utilize programs that allow students to manipulate material with a stylus or use touchscreen technology. Such manipulation enables students to interact directly with a lesson.

Clickers allow students to choose an answer from a teacher-generated assessment projected on a Smart Board. Implementation of such technology creates an environment where students should be effectively listening to direct instruction in order to respond to the presented questions correctly. Additionally, these types of assessments give teachers immediate data on their students' levels of understanding. Scores from these types of assessments may be linked directly to an electronic gradebook, allowing the teachers an easy way to collect grades. Information collected through such assessments can then be used to create intervention groups.

Of course, the use of standard conventions of the English language is important for all the elements of reading and writing. A demonstration of grammar usage throughout assessments is critical. Vocabulary, clarity, and expression should all be used to determine the adequate assessment of a student's response.

Students should respond to reading assessment questions by using evidence from the text—whether that text is informational or literary. In the past, students used personal experience or prior knowledge to respond to questions. Reading lessons and teachers are now using text-dependent questions within assessments. In order to perform well on such assessments, students should be actively engaged in the lesson and text. Students should extract information directly from the source when answering questions and find details based on evidence from the text. Even inferences should be supported by text evidence to support answers. During the evaluation of such assessments, teachers should confirm that an idea was indeed taken from the text itself.

Assessments can be formative or summative. **Formative assessments** include formal and informal procedures done throughout a unit of study, such as observations, exit tickets, individual whiteboards, or student portfolios. Teachers use formative assessments in order to gauge whether or not additional instruction for a particular skill is required. **Summative assessments** are usually done at the end of a unit and are considered to be high-stakes. Summative assessments are sometimes standardized, which yields a high degree of accuracy in the data. They might also be authentic or task-based, such as a portfolio, which offers teachers a strong understanding of the students' abilities and growth.

Whether formative or summative, assessments should be given frequently and purposefully. This will indicate which students need intervention and which students can be given more independent practice. Frequent assessments help teachers tackle reading difficulties before they become overwhelming. If an instructor waits too long to assess a child, it is more difficult to identify the exact skill with which a student requires intervention. When assessments are given frequently, teachers can readily identify student difficulties in order to provide immediate intervention. This, in turn, increases the chances that a skill is mastered by all students.

Using a systematic approach to reading instruction will help teachers address concerns early on and help them ensure that all students have demonstrated a sufficient level of mastery of particular skills at designated points. Systematic reading approaches should include direct and explicit instruction while giving students opportunities to show what they have learned. Skills should be broken down into smaller units of information in order to allow students to grasp a concept. Such techniques allow students to synthesize smaller concepts into a larger schema. The implementation of mini-lessons allows teachers to intervene and give remediation throughout a unit before a larger skill is introduced. In this way, a solid foundation is developed on which students can later build more complex and higher-order thinking skills.

In conclusion, instruction should be differentiated to address the variety of learners in the classroom. Instruction should allow for high expectations at each child's learning level. Ongoing assessments will guide an instructor as to which students will benefit from independent practice versus those students who need more remediation.

Instructing and Advising Teachers to Differentiate Reading Instruction

<u>Key Factors to Consider in Planning Differentiated Reading Instruction</u>
The following are key factors to consider in planning differentiated reading instruction:

- Assess knowledge and skills in the specific area(s) of reading.
- Identify the prerequisite skills that are required for students to benefit from instruction.
- Properly pace the instruction of such skills.
- Understand the complexity of the skills and content that should be presented.
- Provide scaffolding to ensure that all students can access higher-level reading knowledge and skills.

The breakdown of materials and standards over a week is vital. A weeklong reading lesson can be broken down into five sections or days. Skills presented throughout the course of the lesson can be assessed at the end of the week. Teachers can evaluate student advancement more effectively with smaller group sizes. Therefore, initial assessments should be used to differentiate instruction and to group students according to their abilities and skill levels. Students who have mastered the skill(s) can move at a faster pace and on to more complex tasks while working at their seat independently. This gives the instructor time to meet with students who need more remediation and teacher direction. Students who need the most help should meet with the teacher individually for scaffolded remediation of less-complex tasks. Struggling students also benefit from slower-paced lessons and additional practice.

The anchor standards for college and career readiness include key ideas and details, craft and structure, and integration of knowledge and ideas:

1. **Ideas and details:** Students must be able to make inferences and draw conclusions from a text, determine central ideas and themes, and analyze how authors develop individuals, events, and ideas throughout the text.

2. **Craft and structure:** Students will need to interpret figurative meanings, analyze how parts of a text relate to each other, and assess points of view.

3. **Integration of knowledge and ideas:** Students must evaluate content across a variety of media and formats.

<u>Managing Differentiated Reading Instruction to Meet the Needs of all Students</u>
The following are ways for educators to organize and manage differentiated reading instruction and interventions to meet the needs of all students:

- Use flexible grouping, individualized instruction, and whole-class instruction as needed.

- Use all components of their state's adopted materials to make grade-level content accessible for all students.

- Create intervention groups according to the severity of student needs.

Reading instruction begins with daily whole-class lessons that are conducted to introduce new skills. The remaining time of a reading lesson should be dedicated to independent practice for those who have mastered the skill and intervention time for students who are progressing towards the skill.

Lessons should utilize materials adopted by the practitioner's own state. These materials have been evaluated for consistency with the state's standards and benchmarks. Materials that have been evaluated by one's own state include textbooks, technology-based resources, curriculum sets, and tests. Thus, there are enough materials to use with all types of learners to ensure accessibility for all students.

Students should be assessed during daily lessons. Formative assessments can be done on a daily basis through informal observations. Summative assessments can be done weekly. The teacher ought to use student performance on such assessments to organize the students into smaller intervention groups. The organization of such groups helps to ensure that all students are provided with differentiated interventions on the exact skills in which they struggle. Students who display difficulty in a skill should meet with a teacher for one-on-one or small-group remediation more frequently than students who have mastered the skill. These latter students will be given more independent work at their seats. Groups can be changed accordingly as students' performance changes.

Professional Development

Instruction methodologies and research into learning development are constantly changing, so keeping up to date on this information is essential to ensuring students get the most out of their education. Reading instructors should always be open minded to ways they can enhance the quality of their reading program. Professional development will also enable teachers to do their job with more ease while also opening up future opportunities. Several accredited programs are offered online and can be taken as a part of a formal professional development program. In addition to taking more advanced teaching and subject-related courses, there are multiple ways an individual specialist can enhance their knowledge base.

If a specialist is relatively new to teaching, one of the simplest forms of professional development is to shadow other professionals and get their teaching advice. An instructor can also have fellow teachers sit in on their class and critique their teaching style in order to improve instruction. Conferences and webinars offer a broad range of topics and experts from which to draw further insight. Instructors will have options to learn from a variety of sources and get the chance to have pressing questions addressed. In addition to developing teaching skills at such events, reading instructors also take away contacts they can then follow up with. For example, a reading specialist may meet another experienced teacher working with dyslexic students. When this reading specialist receives students with dyslexia, the reading specialist can reach out to the expert for teaching advice or resources to help these students.

Attending teacher workshops is a great way to sharpen specific skill sets such as classroom management or differentiating lesson plans. This is a great time to ask questions and engage with workshop leaders about research topics. Workshops are also very proactive, so dialogue and one-on-one feedback tend to be more prominently featured than in larger conferences.

One minor way of enhancing one's reading teaching skills is by joining a book club or focused reading session. Not only will this be an opportunity to practice communication skills, but also a chance to discover new materials to either use in class or read for professional development.

Reading Curriculum

There can be a lot of textual and lesson variety in a given curriculum; however, there should be an overarching purpose within the design of the course or unit. Instructors must design curriculum in a way that highlights specific knowledge and skills. By the end of the course, students should be able to achieve key goals and deliverables that indicate that the instruction was insightful and successfully delivered. This is very important for helping students gain the skills needed to progress to more difficult levels of education as well as preparing for their eventual careers.

The **backward design approach** to curriculum design looks first at the end of the course—the results of the instruction—in order to inform the implementation of the lessons. Once the lesson goals are established, instructors can then plan how they will be achieved. This starts with identifying evidence of student progress. These can be tests or other assessments, discussions, and even graded papers. The goal in this stage is to gain concrete signs of whether or not the material is successfully helping students reach the lesson goals or if the material needs to be modified to do so. This may also reveal a need for special instruction for individuals who are struggling. Finally, the reading curriculum needs to have teaching methods that will enable the instructor to assess skills while also striving toward reaching the primary skill-set goals. Lessons must be conducted in a way that progressively strengthens and develops the skills students need to achieve the curriculum priorities. Instructors should consider activities, plan lectures, and select reading materials that will align with the course goals. Lesson materials should be challenging but engaging, motivating students to test their skills and seek to expand them.

When the overall goals and layout of the program are established, being able to plan everyday lessons becomes easier and more flexible. While remaining focused on reaching the end goals of the program, certain areas of the curriculum can be focused on more or less, depending on the needs of the students. If one teaching method proves successful during one stage of the curriculum, it can be enhanced and used again later on.

Promoting Reading Development through Environment

Creating a Literacy-Rich Environment
Projects and presentations are great ways to create a literacy-rich environment where reading is promoted. Projects and presentations should also meet the speaking and writing components of the framework for ELA in the state where the reading instructor works. Thirdly, projects and presentations encourage students to use reading and research as an avenue through which they can set and pursue personal goals.

Presentations can include digital and technology components, such as PowerPoint®, Glogster, Powtoon, or recorded videos. Projects may be presented as a "grab bag" or tic-tac-toe board that include several options that students can choose to complete. In this way, students can pick projects that meet their individual abilities, goals, and interests. Allowing students to choose from a set group of options also promotes differentiation within a class.

Rather than utilizing reading groups, students can be arranged into book clubs, author studies, literature circles, or other discussion groups. All members of such groups can read the same text together or independently. Either way, the group's members or entire class should come together at some point each week to discuss the selected text.

Support Systems Available to Promote Skillful Teaching of Reading
Professional development (PD) opportunities are often used to expose teachers to strategies that can be used to promote skillful teaching of reading. Sometimes administrators offer incentives for teachers to attend after-school PD courses. Such incentives may include extra pay, credits to advance degrees or salary, or free materials and resources. If money is a factor, schools may be able to receive tuition compensation when teachers take courses that are specific to the schools' goals. Either way, PDs enable teachers to collaborate with coworkers or teachers from other grade levels and/or schools in order to learn from one another.

Grade-level teams and meetings are other ways that teachers can sit down with peers to share materials, ideas, and resources. If students within a grade level are struggling with a particular standard, it is more economical and efficient to address this concern across a grade level. Grade-level teams may be able to order materials with provided funds or grants to enhance their students' learning in reading. There are many resources and books that are directly related to reading state standards and benchmarks. Similarly, workloads can be split up amongst members of the team. Rather than each teacher finding materials for several standards, each member of the team can locate materials for a specific standard with which the majority of the team's students struggle.

Some schools employ a **reading coach** who specializes in ELA and content standards. A primary role of reading coaches is to be trained in reading interventions in order to provide teachers the strategies needed to ensure their students meet annual growth expectations of select benchmarks. In order to become specialists in such reading processes, reading coaches attend district-wide meetings to learn about resources, strategies, and curriculum changes. Reading coaches are great advocates when it comes to getting resources. They help schools and/or districts select texts, leveled readers, and matching assessments. Reading coaches also train and educate teachers in how to use such resources effectively within their classrooms. Sometimes, reading coaches even teach lessons, help with small groups, or assess students.

Collaborating with Members of Educational Community

Addressing the Goals of the Reading Program

Teaching is inherently a collaborative process. In addition to working with students and learning together as a class, a reading specialist can seek assistance from fellow staff and involve individual families with their child's education. Working with community figures can also broaden a reading specialist's skill set while enhancing his or her ability to provide high-quality, well-rounded instruction.

Being a reading specialist on staff at school doesn't isolate the individual to one classroom or a single subject. Quite the opposite. While a reading instructor has a central education focus, their insight on reading and communication learning can benefit teachers in many other departments. For example, if a math teacher has a student struggling with a particular concept, a reading instructor can offer advice on how to assess where communication disconnects may lie. The issue may be related to reading comprehension or a purely math-related issue, but the reading instructor can still help work with the math instructor on explaining the concept in an alternative way to garner results. On the other hand, a reading instructor can benefit from the different methods of content instruction or assessment practices used by other instructors. Collaborating with other teachers enables the reading specialist to basically assist not only students in their classroom but students in other classes. Teaching staff should be seen as a team with the shared goal and responsibility of providing students with great education in all of their subjects.

Like working with fellow teachers, a reading instructor should also feel comfortable reaching out to administrative staff, the community, and parents for support. Because the instructor can't be everywhere at once, these people are key for providing valuable insight on individual students and also helping them with their education outside of class. School administrative professionals can provide information on behavioral issues or give feedback on a student's communication/interactions that can help instructors isolate core issues and adjust instruction. Parents can do this also, but because they are at home with the student, they can actually reinforce teaching methods for homework. This, in turn, will lead to more support and a concentrated effort from the parents to assist their children with everyday writing and communication scenarios too, providing additional lessons outside of the classroom. On a grander scale, community events are a great way for students to listen to proper language and practice applying their language skills in real-world scenarios.

Consensus Building and Conflict Resolution

When teaching a classroom of adolescents, there are bound to be conflicts that need to be addressed. Sometimes conflict can be with instructors or administration, or even parents, regarding the direction of the program. This conflict doesn't necessarily reflect on the reading specialist but perhaps strategies and subject matter within the course. It's important for specialists not to get offended, but to remember that the ultimate goal is to educate students in the best ways possible. Sometimes changing aspects of reading programs to address key issues is necessary; however, it's also important for reading specialists to maintain practices that will help students gain reading proficiency. Sometimes confusion or issues arise simply because people are unaware of the program's goals or internal structures.

Asking questions and providing detailed, professional responses is key to addressing any questions about the program or reading material choices. Explaining the overall goal of the program and/or the specific approach to address key issues is important to clarify why reading programs are conducted the way they are. Reaching a resolution begins with establishing a common understanding between two parties. A specialist should ask why there are concerns, clarify specific problems, and inquire if there are suggestions to address them. Discussion is very important; perhaps there are minor concerns that can be easily corrected or suggestions to improve instruction that benefit both the instructor and the students.

When defending key lesson choices, it is important to not be defensive and to be open-minded to improvement. Providing assessment results and gathering insight from other instructors and even students can add beneficial evidence that supports the program's design.

Sometimes changes are requested to be made as a way to reach a resolution, but this is not necessarily a bad thing. These compromises take into mind professional opinions and research that could positively impact the growth of both students and instructors alike. It is important for the reading specialist to keep the core fundamentals of the reading program, but perhaps incorporating additional materials and new approaches will enhance the overall program. Consensus can be built by illustrating the importance of core reading and language development tenants but also by acknowledging the validity of the new perspectives. If these core aspects are questioned, the instructor can elaborate on their importance and role. Being resolute but open to change is an ideal stance for the reading instructor to take.

Relevant Research Findings

As a reading specialist instructor, it is important to not only educate students but also to further the knowledge base of other teachers and educators. New research on learning disabilities, teaching techniques, and even psychological research is very valuable to any educational institution. This new information will impact the overall instruction of students throughout departments and potentially influence funding opportunities. Because research is constantly producing new ideas and improvements, educational institutions that incorporate it will continue their strive toward excellence. Therefore, it is important to offer the highest quality of information possible.

New information is only as good as its quality and authenticity. It is important to investigate all new research carefully, and make sure the sources are credible. Assessing the findings and claims of other professionals is important as well. If the information doesn't make sense or is poorly documented, reading specialists should consider researching the same material from a different source. When drawing from official research documentation, one must check bibliographies or specific incidents mentioned to fact-check the writer's claims. Not only does this new research impact the individual reading specialist, but also the students and the institution's integrity. Reading specialists must also be aware of trends within the research and whether the research in question is attempting to support a specific agenda or theory. Being mindful of opposing viewpoints in research topics will enable a reading instructor to offer balanced information that addresses topics.

Educational research can be quite difficult to understand and apply. When presenting information to peers, the specialist must use clear language and be prepared to address questions. Being able to present this material necessitates more than just knowledge of the research; one must be able to apply it to the current programs, or at least present ideas on how to do so. Reading instructors should ask themselves: Can this research help address current program issues? Can this research accelerate or improve student learning? Can these methodologies be seamlessly integrated, or will there be problems adjusting program parameters? Such analysis will not only determine whether the research in question has good information but also whether it's appropriate for the current needs of the school, faculty, and students.

Communicating with Policymakers, the Media, and the General Public

Advocating for positive change and support of literacy is an essential role of reading specialists. Essentially, this means educating the public and key figures in society about the importance of reading education in order to garner support for programs within the school as well as research. It is through advocacy by educators and other experts that people become aware of key issues within education and are moved to aid instructors in their mission to enhance the lives of students through literacy. Instructors can do this in several ways, but primarily it is through speaking engagements with other people.

Some of the most important people to seek advocacy from are elected officials and policymakers who establish rules and regulations of state and county education. These individuals can range from senators, governors, and even members of the State Departments of Education. These people are elected to serve the best interest of their constituents, so it is the job of the reading specialist to show how reading education efforts are in the people's interest. This can be done by presenting research on how reading impacts child development and career opportunities. Instructors can also highlight their own work within the classroom, sharing the accomplishments of individual students. Instructors can also write letters to officials or attend official school board events to promote key programs.

The **public**—people who include ordinary citizens—is also important to enhancing education. After all, it's the public who ultimately elects policymakers and controls the rules of the land. Advocating how reading and literacy empower children to reach their potential is an important step in gaining the attention needed to make valuable change for education. Community support is also what will help create fundraisers and similar events needed to raise school funding for programs and structural projects. The public might not know a lot about the role of literacy in early development, so sharing information on the subject will demonstrate that their investment in education is well funded. Engaging with the public also helps parents and family members be aware of learning issues and can open up dialogues that will lead to more children receiving valuable resources and instruction.

Presenting one's voice in the media will also gain advocacy, whether through writing or commenting on Web articles or sharing views on literacy through social media. Web networking is a great way to tell people on a grand scale how important reading education is for America's youths. Instructors and literacy advocates should not be afraid to address issues by commenting on video or written posts that seem to be contrary to educational values. Instructors should also encourage other staff to be active online, sharing their knowledge and passion for education.

Partnerships Between Schools and Community Agencies

As mentioned, advocating literacy is highly important to sustaining the value and role of education throughout the country. To this extent, no one can enhance educational programs alone. Schools are tied to the communities they are a part of, so it is through generous funding and support from community agencies that schools are able to continue their impact on education. Therefore, cultivating partnerships between local schools and the community is essential on many levels. Not only will this help gain support for key programs, it also serves to get parents and key community figures involved in the education process.

Being proactive in the community will help when seeking which groups may be interested in collaboration. Reading specialists should look for partners that share similar values, such as promoting reading, education, or outreach. Common places where people gather, such as a community gym or even a theater company, are ideal because both depend on the community being proactive and prosperous. For example, an independent theater company is a great place to promote literacy programs because plays are both a dramatic and written art form. Organizing a collaborative partnership could bring positive attention to both groups. The students' program would be highlighted and garner support, while the theater company would gain more attention, not only for their performances but also for giving back to the community. Partnerships can be established by any kind of agency, from local charities to large or small businesses.

Connecting with the community is key; one has to engage potential partners in order to assess whether a collaboration can even be possible. Maintaining contact lists will enable the reading specialists to have a pool of potential groups to reach out to and partner with at all times. It is also important to have a clear form of collaboration in place. Will the partner in question sponsor an event, hand out pamphlets on the importance of reading, or host a field trip? Planning collaborative efforts in advance is essential to both parties.

Practice Questions

1. It is important to choose a variety of texts to elicit higher-level thinking skills. Which of the following text groupings would be appropriate to reach this goal?
    a. Basal readers, fantasy texts, and sci-fi novels
    b. Nonfiction, fiction, cultural pieces, and United States documents
    c. Scholastic magazine articles
    d. Textbooks and high-interest blogs

2. Informational text should comprise what percentage of all text used in instruction by the time students reach the twelfth grade?
    a. 25 percent
    b. 55 percent
    c. 50 percent
    d. 70 percent

3. A teacher wants to help her students write a nonfiction essay on how the Pueblos built their homes. Before they write, she helps the students make clay from corn starch and water, draw a plan for the house with a ruler, and build it using the clay and leaves from the schoolyard. These exercises are examples of what?
    a. Proficiency
    b. Collaboration
    c. Constructive writing
    d. Cross-curricular integration

4. A first grader that is in a classroom's reading center appears to be frustrated. How can the teacher best help this student find a book that is at the appropriate reading level?
    a. Have the student do a five-finger test for vocabulary
    b. Pick a new book for the student
    c. Have the student try to figure it out on their own
    d. Have a peer read the book to the student

5. Which element is important for a teacher to consider when planning a lesson?
        I. Pacing
        II. Intervention groups
        III. Modeling and direct instruction
    a. III only
    b. I and II
    c. I and III
    d. I, II, and III

6. What is an effective strategy when working with a child who has an Individualized Education Program (IEP)?

    I. Provide remediation during which the teacher works with the student on a particular skill

    II. Allow the student to work independently

    III. Chart the student's performance on a particular skill on a weekly basis in order to observe the student's growth over time

    a. II and III

    b. I and II

    c. I and III

    d. I, II, and III

7. Which trait teaches students to build the framework of their writing?

    a. Conventions

    b. Word choice

    c. Ideas

    d. Organization

8. What is the goal of a reading specialist position at a school site?

    I. To inform staff of changes in the curriculum

    II. To offer reading lessons in the classroom

    III. To instruct staff on how to do their job

    a. II only

    b. I and II

    c. II and III

    d. I, II, and III

9. Which of the following is NOT the best way to utilize a reading center or corner in a classroom?

    a. As a spot for students to play games

    b. As a private and quiet place to chat about books

    c. As a location to provide a variety of leveled readers

    d. As fun and entertaining décor to enhance a comfortable learning environment

10. Which trait is most commonly associated with giving individuality and style to writing?

    a. Voice

    b. Word choice

    c. Presentation

    d. Ideas

11. What types of questions should be offered in an assessment in order to check for its validity?

    a. Open-ended questions only

    b. Selected-response questions

    c. Both open-ended questions and multiple-choice questions

    d. None of these

12. Which trait ultimately forms the content of the writing?

    a. Conventions

    b. Word choice

    c. Ideas

    d. Voice

13. If the majority of students in the classroom did not master a skill, what is the next step that a teacher should take?

    a. Reteach the skill to the entire class

    b. Break the class into smaller groups to remediate the skill

    c. Have students mediate with each other about the skill

    d. Move on to the next skill because time is critical

14. What nonfiction texts can be used to teach reading standards?

        I. United States documents

        II. Magazines for pleasure

        III. Science and social studies textbooks

    a. III only

    b. II and III

    c. I and III

    d. I, II, and III

15. When selecting and organizing intervention groups, which of the following is most important?

    a. Organizing students according to their level

    b. Organizing students according to their grades on their prior report cards

    c. Organizing students according to the opinions of the students' previous teachers

    d. Organizing students according to their behavior in the classroom

Answer Explanations

1. B: Students should read a wide variety of literary and informational texts to prepare for college. Texts may extend across a wide variety of genres, timelines, and cultural works. Nonfiction, fiction, cultural pieces, and United States documents are all excellent examples of texts to use during reading instruction.

2. D: Students should be exposed to 70 percent of nonfiction text during reading instruction by the time they reach the twelfth grade. By eighth grade, students should be exposed to 55 percent of nonfiction text. Students should be exposed to a 50/50 balance from kindergarten to fifth grade.

3. D: Cross-curricular integration is choosing to teach writing projects that include the subjects of science, social studies, mathematics, reading, etc.

4. A: Young students should use the five-finger test to select an appropriate-level text. Using the five-finger test, a student selects a page within a text that he or she wants to read. The student holds up a finger for each word he or she is unable to read on that page. If the student has five fingers up after reading the entire page, then the student should stop and choose a book at an easier reading level. If there are not a variety of books of various reading levels from which a student can choose, then the student is likely to become frustrated. Such frustration may cause the student to stop reading for pleasure and see reading as a chore.

5. D: Elements of a good lesson are all of the listed criteria. Pacing, modeling, direct instruction, and intervention are necessary to build a strong reading lesson. Teachers need to account for time given by a district for reading. That time should include whole-class instruction of new reading skills. Teachers should then assess students formatively during guided and independent practice in order to break students into groups based on their performance levels.

6. C: It is important for teachers to allocate time to work one-on-one with students who have IEPs. Students with IEPs may need to have skills retaught. Measuring the growth of students with IEPs can be done by charting their performance levels on a weekly basis. If there is little or no growth, a teacher may need to revisit his or her pacing or the form of instruction being used with the student(s).

7. D: Organization is the trait that teaches students how to build the framework of their writing. Students choose an organizational strategy or purpose for the writing and build the details upon that structure. There are many purposes for writing, and they all have different frameworks.

8. B: The role of a reading specialist is not to tell teachers how to do their jobs, but rather to assist them. One role of a reading coach is to help teachers in their classrooms with assessing students or even teach lessons for teachers. Another role of a reading specialist is to inform staff of district changes at staff meetings, in-services, or in professional development opportunities. Such changes may include alterations of curriculum or state standards.

9. A: A reading corner is not designed to be a "hang out" for students. Rather, it is a place for students to share thoughts on books or discuss recommendations. A reading corner should have a fun atmosphere to enhance students' interest in reading and be filled with a variety of genres and levels.

10. A: Voice is the primary trait that shows the individual writing style of an author. It is based on an author's choice of common syntax, diction, punctuation, character development, dialogue, etc.

11. C: In order to check assessments for validity, it's important to understand what both question types entail for students. Selected-response questions cover a broad range of topics in a shorter period of time. However, students can guess the correct response on selected-response questions. For example, a typical multiple-choice question provides four answers from which a student can choose. This gives students a 25 percent chance of guessing the correct answer. Therefore, the results of select-response assessments are not always valid. Open-ended questions are longer and more time-consuming. However, these questions assess students' skill levels more effectively. Open-ended assessments also allow students to use text-based evidence to support their answers.

12. C: Ideas ultimately form the content of the writing. The Ideas Trait is one of the 6+1 Traits model and is where students learn to select an important topic for their writing. They are taught to narrow down and focus their idea before further developing it.

13. A: If the majority of the class did not master a skill taught, then the best plan is to reteach the skill to the entire class again. To break the class into intervention groups would not be the best use of time. Also, if many students did not understand the skill, then perhaps the skill was not properly taught the first time. A different teaching approach may need to be used. The utilization of different types of media, more direct instruction, and modeling of the skill should be done several more times before the students are assessed on the skill a second time.

14. C: Good reading strategies are essential for all subject areas across the curriculum. In order to excel in science and social studies, there needs to be a good reading foundation—especially in nonfiction texts. The United States documents or science and social studies textbooks may all be used to teach nonfiction. Informational magazines may have good nonfictional material, but these need to be selected carefully, to ensure that the reading is appropriately substantive. Basal readers are also good examples of nonfiction text.

15. A: Intervention groups should be organized based on student performance. Although the behavior of students may be taken into consideration, the organization of group members should be primarily based on each student's performance levels.

Professional Learning and Leadership

Organizing a Written Response to a Topic Relating to the Development of Student Literacy

In addition to researching new education methods and discoveries, reading specialist candidates should be comfortable writing about their field. Whether it's new research, an analysis of a particular class, or a status report, it's important to utilize good writing skills. The writing should be detailed and yet as concise as possible. Using clear, easy-to-understand language will ensure that all readers will be able to grasp the material properly. It's important to focus on the specific subject matter at hand and not deviate; instead, reading specialists should elaborate on relevant points and why they matter.

When writing about student literacy, it's important to distinguish research or accepted views, observations, and opinions. Just like with a student's composition, any claim made regarding the profession of literary instruction should be corroborated with supporting information. For example, if there is a specific learning disability being addressed, it would be useful to describe specific indications of this issue and how this impacts the cognition of reading. Then, after establishing this base information, an instructor can describe its relevance—how it applies to their current work. Providing detailed observations will also be useful.

When documenting observations, it is important to not only note key areas of difficulty or potential learning disorders but also strategies for improvement. Providing a plan of how to address these issues will enable the instructor to learn appropriate teaching methods and set goals for the student. Assessment results can be documented as well. By showing successive assessments, the writer can illustrate patterns that indicate reading issues and/or show student progress after differentiated instruction.

Analyzing core issues in literacy development shows an in-depth knowledge of how reading is learned in relation to adolescent cognition. To do this effectively, candidates should be able to address the stages of development and assess a student's current stage. Addressing other concepts, such as the effect of culture and perspective, can also play a role in responses. These are also factors that can cause misinterpretation of reading materials or simply produce an alternate interpretation. Therefore, these differences should be elaborated on to eliminate any confusion.

Analysis of Individual Student Case Study

Prepare an Organized Written Response to a Case Study of an Elementary Student

A **case study** is a formal written analysis that has a clear overarching purpose. A case study on an individual elementary student focuses on the individual in question and examines his or her learning issues and progress throughout instruction. The case study documents specific reading issues and solutions in order to learn from this individual study to help future instructors and students. It's also crucial to have a clear timeline of progress throughout the study.

Case studies should open with the student's reading issues. A candidate should explain where the difficulties occurred, such as in speaking challenges, reading struggles, and poor results on assessments. This establishes the focus of the study to help the student overcome issues by improving instruction. Sometimes, there are no issues to solve in a study. If this is the case, a study can focus on new teaching strategies, such as the introduction of a new study resource or lesson structure. In this scenario, the candidate should begin with why the new methods are being applied and the goals of these new strategies—perhaps to improve reading instruction while boosting class engagement.

After introducing the root problem or question of the case study, there needs to be data. Candidates should document the steps taken to address the causes of the issues. Describing the methodologies used for pinpointing specific areas of reading confusion will clarify where and why the issues are occurring. From here, it's time to document the prescribed instruction modifications used to get the student up to speed. In addition to writing how and why differentiated instruction was used to help the student, the candidate should also describe the results of teaching alterations. If the first round of differentiated instruction doesn't help, the instructor should describe this and then explore why this was so. The writer should also discuss how teaching methods then changed again to become more effective. When new instruction takes effect and the student improves, the outcome should also be written about to clearly Illustrate the results. Improvements are very important in these case studies and will help establish successful methods for future reading instruction.

Constructed Response

Constructed Response 1

Prepare an Organized Written Response to a Topic Relating to the Development of Student Literacy.

Mr. Brown is a reading specialist at Carroll High School and assists several teachers and classes with literacy development skills. While most students seem to be writing well, Mr. Brown notices that several students in the classes seem to have trouble reading written words. These children come from a wide range of backgrounds, including native and non-native English speakers.

Task 1: What are some ways Mr. Brown can assess the students' skill levels to determine where the root of their reading issues lie?

Task 2: Describe how Mr. Brown can guide the instructors in addressing the reading issues with differentiated instruction.

Constructed Response 2

Prepare an Organized Written Response to a Case Study of an Elementary Student.

The Scenario:

The following case study is focused on Caleb, a second-grade student. Caleb's primary instructor has noticed that when Caleb reads material aloud in class, he will often take long pauses and read the sentences slower than the other students. This sometimes causes him to stutter or hesitate during longer sentences. Another issue is that sometimes he will switch the order of the words he sees, for example, putting the word *the* after the word *cat* in a sentence. Despite this, Caleb is very bright and seems to fully grasp the context of the material. He also appears to be engaged when answering questions but is hesitant when having to read in front of the class. Caleb's teacher has requested that Mr. Breiner, the reading specialist, evaluate Caleb to understand what might be causing his issues. While Caleb is highly intelligent, the teacher is wondering whether his problems with reading may indicate a reading disorder. Whatever is delaying Caleb's reading, Mr. Breiner has been requested to present ideas on how to help Caleb's reading skills improve. The teacher wants to be able to learn how to address reading issues like Caleb's in the future, or at least be able to identify core literary issues very early in the developmental stage.

Using the information in the scenario and the document below, write a response in which you apply your knowledge of literacy assessment and instructional strategies to analyze this case study. Your response should completely address the following tasks:

Teacher notes:

- When reading the sentence, "The next-door neighbors adopted the cat that had been homeless," Caleb switched *the* and *cat*. He also seemed to take longer to sound out *homeless*.

- Longer sentences seem to cause Caleb confusion when reading aloud.

- In some of his writing responses, Caleb will sometimes switch the letters within the words or the words themselves.

- Caleb understands material clearly and gives insightful thoughts aloud. No speech problems were observed.

Task 1: Identify methods of observation that may indicate whether or not Caleb has a learning disorder. What kind of assessments can be used to determine if his reading difficulties are tied to specific written English structures or if his pausing indicates other psychological disconnects?

Task 2: Based on Caleb's reading difficulties, what are some teaching strategies that can be used to help him improve? Provide details on why differentiating Caleb's instruction would be a major step in bolstering his reading ability.

Dear Praxis Reading Specialist Test Taker,

We would like to start by thanking you for purchasing this study guide for your Praxis Reading Specialist exam. We hope that we exceeded your expectations.

Our goal in creating this study guide was to cover all of the topics that you will see on the test. We also strove to make our practice questions as similar as possible to what you will encounter on test day. With that being said, if you found something that you feel was not up to your standards, please send us an email and let us know.

We would also like to let you know about other books in our catalog that may interest you.

Praxis Elementary Education Test

This can be found on Amazon: amazon.com/dp/1628454326

Praxis English Language Arts

amazon.com/dp/1628454105

Praxis Social Studies

amazon.com/dp/1628454210

Praxis Mathematics

amazon.com/dp/1628454261

Praxis Core Study Guide

amazon.com/dp/1628454946

Praxis General Science Study Guide

amazon.com/dp/1628454385

We have study guides in a wide variety of fields. If the one you are looking for isn't listed above, then try searching for it on Amazon or send us an email.

Thanks Again and Happy Testing!
Product Development Team
info@studyguideteam.com

Interested in buying more than 10 copies of our product? Contact us about bulk discounts:

bulkorders@studyguideteam.com

FREE Test Taking Tips DVD Offer

To help us better serve you, we have developed a Test Taking Tips DVD that we would like to give you for FREE. This DVD covers world-class test taking tips that you can use to be even more successful when you are taking your test.

All that we ask is that you email us your feedback about your study guide. Please let us know what you thought about it – whether that is good, bad or indifferent.

To get your **FREE Test Taking Tips DVD**, email freedvd@studyguideteam.com with "FREE DVD" in the subject line and the following information in the body of the email:

a. The title of your study guide.

b. Your product rating on a scale of 1-5, with 5 being the highest rating.

c. Your feedback about the study guide. What did you think of it?

d. Your full name and shipping address to send your free DVD.

If you have any questions or concerns, please don't hesitate to contact us at freedvd@studyguideteam.com.

Thanks again!

Made in the USA
San Bernardino, CA
15 May 2019